GEM
Identification

By Robert Webster

 STERLING PUBLISHING CO., INC. NEW YORK

OTHER BOOKS OF INTEREST

Colorful Mineral Identifier
Creating Silver Jewelry with Beads
Creative Enamelling & Jewelry-Making
Make Your Own Rings & Other Things

Mosaics with Natural Stones
Pebble Collecting and Polishing
Seashell Collectors' Handbook and Identifier
Stone Grinding and Polishing

Acknowledgments

The author and publishers are greatly indebted to the following for their help with illustrations: Anglo American Corporation of South Africa Ltd.; Australian Information Services; Australian News and Information Bureau; N. W. Ayer and Son, Inc., New York; Eric Bruton, High Wycombe, England; Christie's of London; Colombia Information Service, New York; Cultured Pearl Association of America; De Beers Consolidated Mines Ltd., London; T. A. Durant Ltd., Bidford-on-Avon, England; Government Information Services, Hong Kong; E. P. Joseph Ltd., London; Kazanjian Brothers, Los Angeles; Carola Klein, Idar Oberstein, W. Germany; S. Leaming, Geological Survey of Canada, Vancouver, B.C.; Martin-Foto, Munich, W. Germany; K. Mikimoto and Co., Ltd., New York; A. Monnickendam Ltd., London; David Neiman, London; A. Ruppenthal, Idar Oberstein, W. Germany and London; The Shell Photographic Unit, London; Smithsonian Institution, Washington, D.C.; Sotheby and Co., London and Zurich; Tele-Press Associates, New York; E. A. Thomson (Gems) Ltd., London.

First published in England under the title "Gems in Jewellery" © 1975 by NAG Press Ltd., London, and Robert Webster. This edition adapted by E. W. Egan for American audiences.

Contents

(Color pages follow pages 32 and 64)

Introduction 5
1. Diamond Mining 7
2. Diamonds As Gems 19
   Synthetics and Simulants
3. Ruby and Sapphire 31
   Rubies . . . Sapphires . . . Star Effects . . .
   Types of Cut . . . Simulants
4. Emerald, Aquamarine and the Beryls . 37
   Emerald Simulants . . . Aquamarine . . .
   Other Beryls
5. The Garnets 42
   Almandite . . . Pyrope . . . Grossular
   Garnet . . . Demantoid Garnet . . .
   Spessartite
6. Topaz and Tourmaline 46
   Topaz Simulants . . . Tourmaline . . .
   Tourmaline Simulants
7. Chrysoberyl and Moonstone . . . 50
   Alexandrite . . . Alexandrite Simulants
   Cat's-Eye . . . Cat's-Eye Simulants . . .
   Moonstone . . . Other Feldspars
8. Zircon and Zoisite 54
   Zoisite
9. Peridot and Spinel 56
   Peridot Simulants . . . Spinel
10. Amethyst and Other Quartzes . . . 59
    Rock Crystal . . . Amethyst . . . Citrine
    . . . Other Colors . . . Quartzite . . .
    Synthetic Quartz
11. Opal 65
    Simulants
12. Some Lesser-Known Gemstones . . 70
    Kunzite . . . Sphene . . . Scapolite . . .
    Andalusite . . . Apatite . . . Axinite . . .
    Benitoite . . . Danburite . . . Diopside
    . . . Phenakite . . . Iolite . . . Enstatite
    . . . Idocrase . . . Euclase . . . Epidote . . .
    Kyanite . . . Fibrolite . . . Kornerupine

. . . Brazilianite . . . Cassiterite . . .
Chrysocolla . . . Smithsonite . . .
Chlorastrolite . . . Thomsonite . . . Zinc-
Blende . . . Staurolite
13. Chalcedony, Agate and Jasper . . . 75
    Chrysoprase . . . Agate . . . Moss Agates
    . . . Other Agates . . . Stained
    Chalcedony . . . Jasper
14. Turquoise 80
    Egyptian Turquoise . . . Iranian
    Turquoise . . . The Aztecs . . . The
    Southwest . . . Properties of Turquoise
    . . . Simulants . . . Birthstones
15. Jades 85
    Nephrite . . . Jadeite . . . Simulants
16. Ornamental Stones 90
    Lapis Lazuli . . . Lapis Simulants . . .
    Rhodochrosite . . . Rhodonite . . .
    Fluorspar . . . Onyx Marble . . .
    Alabaster . . . Serpentine . . . Soapstone
    . . . Meerschaum
17. Gems from the Chemist 95
    Synthetics . . . Glass . . . Plastics . . .
    Composite Stones
18. Pearl 99
19. The Cultured Pearl 105
20. Other Gems from Living Things . . 111
    Amber . . . Jet . . . Coral . . . Tortoise-
    shell . . . Sea Shells . . . Ivory . . . Ivory
    Simulants
21. How Gems Are Tested 116
Gem Identification Charts 119
    White Stones . . . Brown Stones . . .
    Black Stones . . . Colorless Stones . . .
    Green Stones . . . Violet Stones . . . Blue
    Stones . . . Red and Pink Stones . . .
    Orange and Yellow Stones
Index 128

The largest known blue (really dark blue) diamond is The Hope, on exhibit at the Smithsonian Institution in Washington, D.C. Now 44½ carats, it was possibly cut from an Indian diamond of 67 carats.

A lustrous cultured pearl of the finest quality gleams from an elegant setting. Pearl jewels like this are very costly.

Introduction

FROM THE BEGINNING of time human beings decorated themselves with brightly colored objects, or objects which they believed had some strange talismanic power. At first they used easily acquired objects such as the teeth of animals killed in the hunt. Teeth are ivory, a material still popular in the arts today. Brightly hued seeds were sought for personal decoration just as they are by native tribes at the present time and, indeed, by more civilized societies. The lovely pearl was an object first found by early man, probably during his never-ending quest for food.

It is evident that the earliest materials used for decoration were obtained from living things. They were not the lustrous and colorful minerals which we prize so highly today. Minerals were first found by primitive man probably as brightly colored pebbles in the river beds or among the broken debris at the foot of mountains, or perhaps some rift in the rocks exposed beautiful well-formed crystals, colorless and colored. Man learned how to shape and form some organic materials but the minerals were so hard he had to use them in their native state, although some time later he mastered the art of drilling stones so that they could be strung and used as pendants or necklaces. There is a trend today to return to the primitive idea and mount these gem materials in their rough stage instead of cutting and polishing them.

Beautiful as many of these natural formations are, the full loveliness of a gem mineral demands that it be cut and polished in order to bring out the full brilliance and luster and the nuances of color. In ancient times there was no fashioning of gemstones by grinding and polishing on the surface a series of plane geometrically-shaped facets in symmetrical arrangement as seen in modern gemstones. It was not until well after the medieval period that this technique evolved. Before then stones were polished with a roughly rounded surface, the forerunner of what is now called the cabochon cut. It is not known when rubies, sapphires and other colored stones were first faceted, and we are forced to relate the date and their treatment to that of the cutting of diamond, which is better documented.

At the turn of the 20th century only a limited number of minerals was used for gemstones in jewelry; and there were far fewer imitations. Today there are many minerals and a great number of artificially produced materials imitating Nature's products.

What constitutes a gemstone? It must be beautiful, for attractiveness is of prime importance; and it must be hard enough to resist the abrasive influences which would tend to destroy its polish. It should also be rare, for rarity implies value and value to many people is an essential criterion. Some stones owe their attractiveness to such effects as the "fire" in a diamond; the play of prismatic colors in an opal; the cat's-eye and star effect seen in some stones, and the "schiller" in moonstone. These effects are not apparent unless the stone is suitably cut and polished.

The intention of this book is to present some facts concerning jewel stones found in a jeweler's shop window, and something about the stones

Three popular styles of ring and cut. A cluster (top left) of brilliant cut diamonds and marquise (boat-shaped) sapphires, a white opal surrounded by diamonds and a marquise-cut topaz set with diamonds.

that can be found in the rough state on beaches, road cuts and in broken rock formations. There is no attempt to describe all the gem materials that have been cut and polished, for the whim of the collector is insatiable and stones have been cut from minerals which often have little or none of the attributes really necessary to be a gemstone. A current problem is with place names because many new republics have changed their original names. In this book some of the new names have been ignored because the older names are still used in gemmology. For example, Ceylon is referred to and not Sri Lanka, and the gemmologist still speaks of Siam rubies, not Thai rubies.

The sophisticated methods used by the professional gemmologist for determining the type of stone, and the scientific aspects of gemstones are not deeply probed here, but some ideas are given as to determining the nature of a stone using only a hand lens and simple gadgets based on easily understood scientific principles. The appendices give pertinent information on the gemstones and are arranged by color, and a list of natal stones is also included.

Wimbledon, 1975   ROBERT WEBSTER

1. Diamond Mining

THE BEST KNOWN GEMSTONE is undoubtedly the diamond. It is the one stone seen in every jeweler's shop window. The diamond has not only a character of its own but a much greater aura of historical associations than other gems. Who is not impressed by the long and gory history of the Koh-i-noor diamond, or the intrigues surrounding the diamond necklace, a jewel in part responsible for bringing Marie Antoinette to the guillotine, or the highly embellished story of the Blue Hope Diamond, which legend says brings ill-fortune to its wearer? The stories of famous diamonds are part of the history of the world.

Diamond has many unique characteristics. Most important of all, it is the hardest substance known to man. In this alone diamond is significant in modern science and in industry. The power of diamond to bend a ray of light is high. Scientists measure this bending power and call it the refractive index of a material. In diamond this power is 2.42, taking that of air as unity. This high refraction, coupled with its hardness, gives diamond its unique surface luster, termed adamantine.

This is not the whole story, for diamond also splits a ray of white light into the rainbow colors of the spectrum. A well-cut diamond displays this fire as flashes of different colored lights.

Diamond is simply crystallized carbon, but so is graphite, one of the softest natural minerals, though the atoms are not nearly so tightly packed in graphite as they are in diamond. The

scientist finds much to interest him in diamond, for it provides many problems which even in this enlightened age are far from resolved. The chemistry of carbon is said to be the chemistry of life. On the other hand, what is livelier than a perfectly fashioned, flawless diamond?

It is not definitely known how diamond is formed in the bowels of the earth. Men of science quite early had the notion that the formation of diamond needed extreme heat and great pressure. During this century P. W. Bridgman proved theoretically that heat and pressure were essential to the formation of diamond and suggested how much of each would be needed. His work inspired others to experiment and finally · produce a synthetic diamond, a true diamond made in a laboratory.

Do natural diamonds form by themselves in the earth at great depth, where temperatures and pressures are high, or is there some other substance involved which helps carbon crystallize as diamond rather than its other form, graphite? We call such a substance, which does not alter itself, but provides the urge for some chemical or crystallographic change, a catalyst. An unknown catalyst might well account for diamond formation.

There is much evidence that diamonds formed in the earth at a depth of some 200 kilometers (120 miles) and that the crystals were carried into the upper layers of the earth's crust by underlying gas pressure through blowholes, or carried

The only large-scale gem mining is for diamonds. This is the head of the Finsch mine in South Africa, a pipe mine where yellow ground containing diamonds is being scooped out. Eventually it will be mined from underground.

by rocks not hot enough to vaporize the crystals or change them into graphite. Therefore diamonds can be expected to be found in blowholes or "pipes." Diamond mining shows that there are such pipes containing diamonds.

It seems clear that the earliest known diamonds were found in the ancient Golconda district of India, between the Kristna and Godivari Rivers in the state of Andhra Pradesh. But it is uncertain when diamonds were first found in India, though many of the historically famous diamonds were early Indian stones. Estimates vary from 800 to 400 B.C., assuming that the stones then described

were true diamonds. The first really authentic report came from the French jeweler and traveler, Jean Baptiste Tavernier, who visited the diamond mines during the 17th century.

The Indian diamonds were recovered from the gravel of dried-up river beds, called alluvial sources, where ancient rivers had brought down minerals from areas far away. As the strength of the river current waxed and waned, the heavier minerals, including diamonds, were dropped to the river bed, or carried along. When the river dried up or changed its course, the minerals deposited on the beds became covered with sand

Topside at Kimberley the ore was sifted by horse-power.

and gravel. The source of these alluvial diamonds found in central India is not known, but they may have come from the pipe near Panna in Madhya Pradesh currently worked for diamonds, or more probably, from undiscovered pipes elsewhere. Alluvial deposits containing diamond around the Landek and other rivers in Borneo are said to have been known since 600 A.D. but are now of little importance.

Before the rich South African deposits were found, the main source of diamonds was Brazil, in the states of Bahia and Minas Gerais. Discovered during the early 18th century, the Brazilian diamonds are found in alluvial gravel called *cascalho*. The present production there is small and the mining poorly organized, as it is carried out by independent diamond diggers called *garimpeiros*. Deposits found in the rivers of Guyana can be thought of as an extension of the Brazilian diamond fields. Miners called by the unusual name "pork-knockers" use primitive tackle to recover the diamonds from inhospitable terrain that is not at all favorable for mining. Nearby Venezuela is another source. The government there seems to be taking some interest in promoting diamond mining but the output is small.

The most important and spectacular diamond find of the 19th century was the alluvial deposits along the Vaal and Orange Rivers in South Africa. Though diamonds were probably known in South Africa before 1866, it was 15-year-old Erasmus Jacob's discovery that year of a bright pebble in the gravels near Hopetown which really started the diamond rush. The pebble proved to be a $21\frac{1}{4}$ carat diamond, later cut into a faceted stone of 10.73 carats. Named Eureka, it was eventually presented to the South African government.

In 1869, a Griqua shepherd boy named Booi found an $83\frac{1}{2}$ carat diamond crystal on a farm in Griqua country, well away from a river. This started a second rush of miners, mainly from the river, or wet diggings, to the new dry diggings, so called owing to their arid surroundings. These dry diggings were in loose yellowish earth, popularly called yellow ground, which changed to a harder blue rock as the miners dug deeper. Most of the miners thought the diamond-bearing earth finished when they reached this different rock. But a more adventurous soul probed deeper into this blue ground and found it even richer in diamond. Later geological and mineral-

The Kimberley Mine or "Big Hole" in South Africa had reached 1,000 feet when this picture was taken in 1876. Before it was shut down in 1960 and water allowed to fill the bottom, it was 3,520 feet deep and 1,520 feet across. It is the largest man-made crater in the world.

ogical examination showed that blue ground and yellow ground alike were essentially the same rock, now called kimberlite. The yellow ground resulted from the weathering and oxidation of the iron in the blue ground.

It was noticed that the dry diggings were usually circular or oval in outline and formed the tops of pipes going deep into the earth. Further, though diamonds were found in the pipes, they were never found in the surrounding rock called the reef. These pipes, of which Jagersfontein was the first to be found, were assumed to be the source of the diamond. But it is now thought that the diamonds were not formed in the kimberlite, but at much greater depths in the earth, and

the kimberlite, acting as a vehicle for the diamonds, was forced up by gas pressure. The alluvial deposits or wet diggings, resulted from the erosion of the pipes in earlier geological times. The diamonds can be carried far from the original pipe which could have been subsequently covered with earth and never discovered.

One kind of alluvial deposit differs from most others. After the rivers have carried the diamonds out into the sea, they have dropped to the sea bed and later been washed up and buried under the sand on the shore. The most important of these deposits are along the shores of South-West Africa around the mouth of the Orange River, which flows into the South Atlantic. The

In Sierra Leone, diamond diggers are panning the diamondiferous gravels of an ancient river bed, now a swamp. The diamonds here are only a few feet below the surface.

diamonds found here undoubtedly come from the pipes around Kimberley. They are mined from the sands and also from the sea bed.

While southern Africa holds the main interest in any study of diamonds, diamonds are also found in quantity in alluvial deposits all over western Africa. Sierra Leone, Ghana, the Ivory Coast, Angola and even inland equatorial Africa and the Congo (Zaïre) are prolific suppliers of alluvial diamonds. The Williamson pipe mine in Tanzania, from which came the beautiful pink diamond owned by Queen Elizabeth II of England, is one which lies outside the general area of pipes. Diamond-bearing pipes have recently been found in Botswana (formerly Bechuanaland).

Diamonds are known to have been obtained from the Ural Mountains in Russia in the 19th century, but little or no systematic mining was ever carried out. Russia produced few diamonds until 1954, when a diamond pipe was discovered by a Russian woman mineralogist in the Yakutia district of Siberia, an area of permanent frost. A number of pipes have since been discovered there and mining, despite the extreme cold, is now carried out most effectively. Diamond mining is now a major industry in Russia.

There are a number of minor sources of diamond in the United States and Australia. Those from Australia are said to be harder than diamonds elsewhere. What appears to be greater hardness may be the result of structural differences which cause knots, making it difficult to cut the stone, just as knots in wood make sawing difficult. Very small diamonds have also been recovered from meteorites.

Prospecting for diamonds was a hit-or-miss procedure in the early days. The miner just chose a promising site, dug down into the gravel and washed it to concentrate the heavy minerals by panning. This concentrate was then searched for diamonds, just as gold miners searched for gold. Prospecting today is more scientific. Trained geologists map the ground and by considering the occurrence of minerals associated with diamonds, track down the diamond deposits.

It is recorded that a Miss Popugayeva discovered the first pipe mine in Siberia, named Zarnitza (Dawn), by tracking back indications given by pyrope garnets, after geologists had observed that the terrain resembled diamond areas in India and Africa. A type of fossil oyster provides an indicator of shore deposits. Another modern technique is to make aerial surveys, photographing the terrain. These aerial pictures can reveal the outline of underlying pipes.

In the early days of diamond mining, the stones

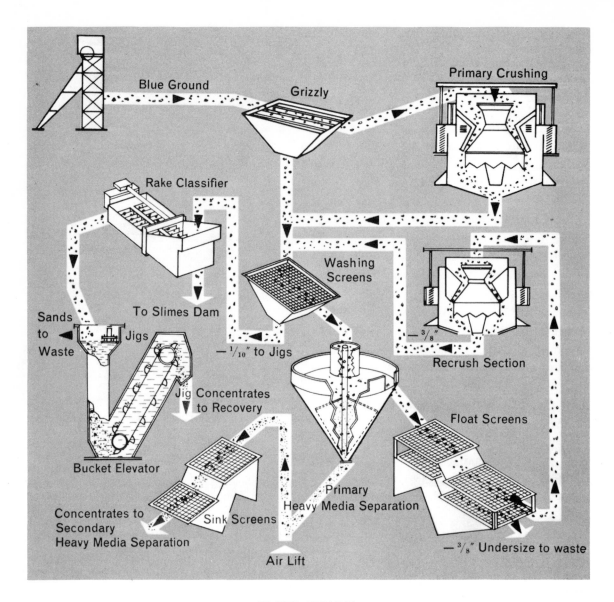

Blue Ground • Grizzly • Primary Crushing • Rake Classifier • Washing Screens • Recrush Section • To Slimes Dam • $-\frac{1}{10}''$ to Jigs • $-\frac{3}{8}''$ • Sands to Waste • Jigs • Jig Concentrates to Recovery • Bucket Elevator • Float Screens • Primary Heavy Media Separation • Concentrates to Secondary Heavy Media Separation • Sink Screens • Air Lift • $-\frac{3}{8}''$ Undersize to waste

FLOW CHART

The blue ground run-of-mine ore is passed over a grizzly to separate the larger lumps, which are later crushed. The smaller material falls through to the washing screens which remove all sand and clay. The minus (smaller than) 1/10-inch material passes to a rake classifier where the fines (small diamond grit) are separated from the sands in a jig. The larger material which has passed over the screens is fed into a chemical-filled (heavy media) cone for gravitational (sink-and-float) separation. The diamondiferous concentrates, being heavier in specific gravity than the chemical, sink and are conveyed over screens again to a secondary heavy media cone for further separation (see next diagram). The material which floats off is rescreened too—the larger lumps to be recrushed and treated, the rest going to waste.

The sink material from the first heavy media separation is further treated in a rotary vessel containing a heavier (in specific gravity) chemical which is still not as heavy as diamond. The part that sinks contains diamonds. This passes directly to the recovery section where it is joined by concentrates which have passed through a jig and both are treated on grease vibrators. The diamonds that adhere to the grease are removed periodically, along with the top layer of grease—the whole layer to go to the water boiler for immersion. The diamonds are freed from the grease and sorted by hand.

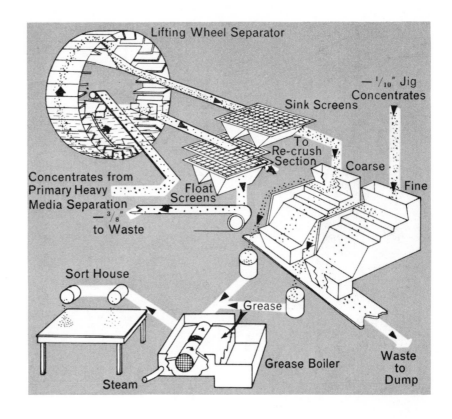

were recovered by sluicing and panning the dug-out gravel with water. The gravel was emptied into sloping wooden troughs crossed by wooden slats, and washed down with water. The lighter particles were carried over the slats, but the heavier concentrate, including the diamonds, was caught in the bars of the slats. In panning, the gravel is washed in a flat conical-shaped dish which is shaken with a circular motion, so that the lighter particles are washed over the edge, leaving the concentrate in the center of the bowl. The concentrate is then spread out on a table and searched for diamonds. The few independent licensed miners left in South Africa use mechanical washers driven by gasoline engines. These washers consist of a circular drum filled with water and gravel, which is stirred up by rotating paddles which swirl the lighter particles of gravel over the edge and concentrate the heavier

minerals at the bottom. These are later removed and searched for diamonds.

There are then three series of processes in diamond recovery: digging the diamond-bearing ground, concentrating the gravel, after breaking up large pieces if necessary, and searching the concentrate for diamonds. Though not very efficient, the methods mentioned were fairly satisfactory for individual miners. In big company operations, the methods are fundamentally the same, but fully mechanized. Before the mines got too deep for surface working, the blue ground was dug out and spread over floors or fields of the veldt to be weathered, helped by watering and plowing. After weathering, the blue ground was concentrated by more sophisticated machinery. Indeed, the final stages of recovering the diamond are largely automatic.

When the pipes had been dug out too deeply

Some diamonds are mined from a thousand feet or more underground by cutting into the pipes of a rock called kimberlite in which the rough diamonds were brought towards the surface from about 120 miles down. A cave is cut in the kimberlite and as the roof caves in the broken rock is dragged out by scrapers like this in the Bultfontein Mine, Kimberley, and hauled to the surface for extraction of diamonds.

for safety and economy, shaft mining in the style of coal mining was introduced. At first a shaft was driven down through the blue ground, but later this idea was abandoned and shafts were sunk in the reef, parallel to the pipe. Horizontal galleries were then driven from this shaft into the kimberlite. Usually two shafts are sunk, one for haulage and the other for ventilation.

There are variations in the arrangement of the horizontal galleries used to excavate the blue ground, such as chambering or stoping. Currently, a complex system works from a ring tunnel surrounding the pipe. The blasted-out rock is pulled out through these drifts by mechanically driven scrapers.

The recovered blue ground is loaded into trucks and sent to crushers. When crushed, the blue ground is retrucked, taken to the haulage shaft and sent to the surface. It is then concentrated in various ways, among them an electrostatic method and a density method using a slurry (a mixture of water and insoluble matter) of a given density, which separates the crushed blue ground into light and heavy groups. The heavy fraction provides the concentrate from which the diamonds are recovered.

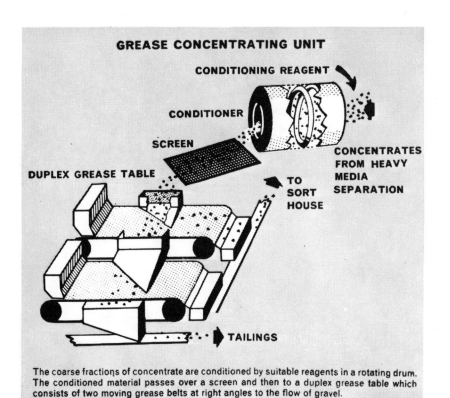

GREASE CONCENTRATING UNIT

CONDITIONING REAGENT

CONDITIONER

SCREEN

DUPLEX GREASE TABLE

TO SORT HOUSE

CONCENTRATES FROM HEAVY MEDIA SEPARATION

TAILINGS

The coarse fractions of concentrate are conditioned by suitable reagents in a rotating drum. The conditioned material passes over a screen and then to a duplex grease table which consists of two moving grease belts at right angles to the flow of gravel.

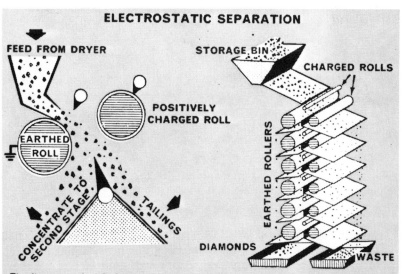

ELECTROSTATIC SEPARATION

FEED FROM DRYER

STORAGE BIN

CHARGED ROLLS

POSITIVELY CHARGED ROLL

EARTHED ROLL

EARTHED ROLLERS

CONCENTRATE TO SECOND STAGE

TAILINGS

DIAMONDS

WASTE

The diagram on the left shows a schematic view of how the fine ($-\frac{1}{4}$") concentrates from the heavy media section are separated when subjected to an electrostatic field of high intensity. The positively-charged roll attracts the more conductive waste minerals, while the diamonds being non-conductive fall straight down a chute. The operation is conducted in six successive stages as shown in the diagram on the right.

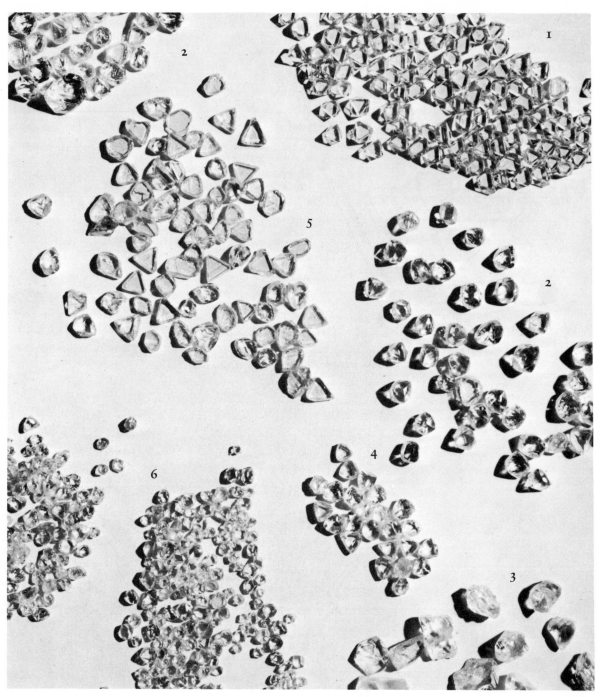

Rough diamonds are found in many shapes and sizes. Those of gem quality have to be faceted to bring out all their glitter. In the rough, diamonds may be octahedral (eight-sided) in shape (1); or they may be irregularly shaped although unbroken (2); if they are broken and blocky they are called cleavages (3); triangular stones or maccles are usually found with a herring-bone line around them (4); they may also be thin but cuttable (5); cleavages weighing less than one carat, known as chips (6), are put into what is known as the melee (or confused mass) along with stones of all shapes weighing under one carat.

At most recovery plants diamonds are recovered from the concentrate by passing it over a vibrating table or a moving belt covered with a layer of grease. Diamond has an affinity for grease but is not easily wetted with water. The concentrate is passed over the grease-laden table in a stream of water, which carries down the non-diamond material as tailings. The diamonds stick to the grease and are later removed from it by boiling. Other forms of separation employ magnetic or electrostatic devices. One modern type of separator is based on the fluorescence of diamonds induced by X-rays.

The recovered diamond crystals do not look at all like the diamonds you see in jewelry. Only a practiced eye would know, by their luster, that they are diamonds. Diamonds from the mines take many forms. Some seem shapeless, others called octahedral crystals are like two four-sided pyramids base to base. Some have 12 faces, but most diamond crystals are multi-faced with as many as 48 faces.

Rough diamonds, as stones from the mines are called, are sent to a Central Sorting Office for classification into grades and colors. Those which are too dark in color, insufficiently well-formed, or too small for cutting into gemstones, are set aside as industrials, for they have many uses in industry. The classification of gem-quality rough diamonds is complex and a task for the expert sorter. The layman, and even the jeweler, rarely sees uncut diamonds, so their grading is not important here.

For practical and economic purposes, nearly all rough diamonds are sold through a Central Selling Organization. When graded and valued, these parcels, as they are called, are only sold to registered diamond buyers, who act as agents for the diamond cutters who shape them into the lovely stones we see in jewelry.

These are finished diamonds in all their beauty. Held in the fingers is a round diamond, the popular brilliant cut. The diagonal row of diamonds are, starting from the left, a pear shape, an emerald cut, an oval and a marquise. The row of round diamonds shows graduated sizes from 20 points (one-fifth of a carat) to a full carat.

2. Diamonds As Gems

DIAMOND CRYSTALS as they are mined are rarely fit for use in jewelry, though in earlier days bright well-formed unpolished octahedral crystals were sometimes set in jewels with the point of the octahedron uppermost. So let us first see how a diamond crystal is cut and polished to produce the lustrous jewel we delight in. Two factors are involved: how can such a hard stone be shaped and polished, and what shape or style of cutting is best used for any particular rough crystal? Let us look at the styles of cutting before describing how they are carried out.

Centuries ago jewelers could only polish an irregular arrangement of facets over the stone with a powder of crushed diamonds, for only diamond will cut and polish diamond. Later the faces of small octahedral crystals were polished and much jewelry of the Renaissance period and the Middle Ages was set with these point-cut stones. This trend was followed by the table-cut style, which simply means that the tip of the octahedron is polished off to produce a square facet at the top.

The old Indian stones cut with facets all over may have inspired the rose-cut style, useful for thin crystals. This cut has a flat base with a pyramidal top covered with from three to 24 symmetrically arranged facets. Many so-called roses used in jewelry today are just chips of diamond polished with a few facets. They are correctly called *senaille*.

The next advance was to polish facets on the corners of table-cut stones, to give a table surrounded by eight facets to form the top of the stone and an equal number of facets below the girdle or setting edge of the stone. This is the single-cut style, which resulted in greater brilliancy. The modern brilliant cut has gradually developed from it.

We now know there is much more to designing the cut of a diamond than placing the facets symmetrically. Diamond is highly reflective, not only externally, but also from inside the back facets. For this reason and for other optical reasons, certain angles between the rear and top facets and the plane of the girdle (dividing edge between the upper set of facets, the crown, and the lower set, the pavilion) must be kept, so that a ray of light entering the front of the stone is wholly reflected through the crown.

The angle of an octahedral crystal is about 55° while the best value for the back facets of a brilliant-cut stone, is 41°, with 34° for the front facets. The crown of the stone should ideally be one-third and the pavilion, or back, of the stone two-thirds the depth of the stone. The reflection of all the light that enters doubles the path, and the colored rays formed when white light travels across two inclined faces are still further separated. These rays may then leave the side facets of the crown as light of different colors, giving the diamond its fire.

A well-cut brilliant has 58 symmetrical facets, including the large central facets called the table and the much smaller *culet* on the point at the back of the stone. This was originally put on to prevent the stone from splintering, but is now often omitted. Present trends have brought in a

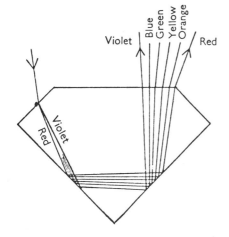

A ray of light striking a top facet of a diamond, is part reflected and part refracted, or bent. The part entering is dispersed into color rays. The result, greatly exaggerated in this diagram, is what is called the diamond's fire, or blaze of color.

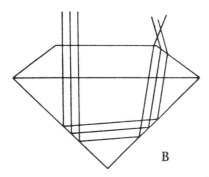

B

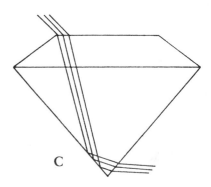

C

Photo and Diagram B show the way the light passes through an ideal cut brilliant diamond after the pavilion has been made to the correct depth. The light comes straight in through the table and out again as fire through the facets of the crown.

Photo and Diagram C show that the pavilion is too deep. Light escapes from the pavilion facets instead of through the crown, thus reducing its brilliance and fire.

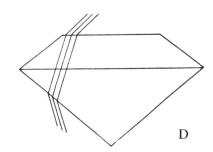

Photo and Diagram D show that the pavilion is too shallow. Light also leaks out of the back.

new style for diamonds, the trap or step cut, which is square or rectangular in outline with mainly rectangular facets. Beveling the four corners of this stone produces the so-called emerald cut. While brilliant-cut stones give the best fire, emerald-cut diamonds have their own special beauty.

Modifications of the trap-cut style produce triangular and lozenge-shaped outlines. Long-shaped stones called *batons* or *baguettes* are often used as supporting stones for so-called single-stone rings and multi-stone jewelry. Brilliant-cut stones need not be round, but can be oval, boat-shaped (called *marquises* or *navettes*), or pear-shaped, when they are known as *pendeloque*. A fine example of the latter is in the Royal Sceptre of the British Regalia. Named the Star of Africa, it is the largest cut diamond in the world, and weighs 530.2 carats. The Swiss cut and single or eight cut have fewer facets than normal.

The earliest method of fashioning diamonds was to rub one diamond against another and use the powder so derived. But how can diamond powder or another diamond be used to cut and polish a diamond when they are both equally hard? The reason is that in a diamond there are differences of hardness in different directions. There are always some surfaces in diamond pow-

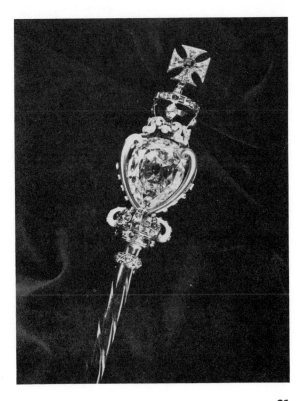

From The Cullinan came The Great Star of Africa, 530.2 carats, the largest cut diamond in existence. It is on view in the Tower of London, as the central portion of the Royal Sceptre.

Some of the Principal Shapes into which Diamonds Are Cut

HEART-SHAPE CUT

JUBILEE CUT

OLD-MINE CUT

DOUBLE-CUT BRILLIANT

PEAR-SHAPE CUT

TWENTIETH-CENTURY CUT

OLD EUROPEAN CUT

TRAP BRILLIANT CUT

EMERALD CUT

SINGLE CUT

OVAL CUT

ENGLISH ROUND-CUT BRILLIANT

MARQUISE or NAVETTE CUT

SQUARE EMERALD CUT

SWISS CUT

SPLIT-BRILLIANT CUT

The square and lozenge cuts date back to medieval times, the rose cut from 1520. In the 16th century, the first brilliant cut was engineered, and as time went on, many ingenious modifications were devised by diamond cutters, as they discovered how best to transform various shapes and sizes of rough diamonds into pools of light and fire.

(from Jewelers' Circular-Keystone)

KEYSTONE CUT

TAPERED PENTAGON CUT

WINDOW CUT

RHOMBOID CUT

DOUBLE-ROSE CUT

STEP-CUT BEAD

BULLET CUT

EPAULETTE CUT

CALF'S-HEAD CUT

WHISTLE CUT

BOAT-SHAPE ROSE CUT

RONDELLE

TRIANGLE CUT

PENTAGON CUT

SHIELD CUT

LONG OCTAGON CUT

PEAR-SHAPE ROSE CUT

TAPERED BAGUETTE

HALF-MOON CUT

TRAPEZE CUT

FAN-SHAPE CUT

CUT-CORNER TRIANGLE CUT

FULL-HOLLAND ROSE CUT

BAGUETTE

MAGNA CUT

LISBON CUT

SEMINAVETTE

LOZENGE CUT

BEVEL CUT

FRENCH CUT

KITE CUT

TABLE CUT

SQUARE CUT

KING CUT

BRAZILIAN CUT

ENGLISH SQUARE-CUT BRILLIANT

LONG HEXAGON CUT

SIX-FACET ROSE CUT

HEXAGON CUT

THREE-FACET ROSE CUT

23

The three largest diamonds ever found all came from Africa. They are the Cullinan (left) weighing 3,106 carats (about 1⅓ lb.) found in 1905, the Star of Sierra Leone, 969 carats, in 1972, and the 995 carat Excelsior found in 1893. They are shown here about half size. The middle one is real and the others models.

der of the harder direction which can grind the softer directions in the stone that is being cut.

Grinding an octahedral diamond to the right form and angles would waste 45 to 50 per cent of the crystal, so cleaving or sawing is resorted to. Like many other crystalline materials, a diamond has lines of comparative weakness along which it may break with fairly smooth surfaces. The four lines of cleavage in diamond lie parallel to the octahedral faces. They are due to planes of weakness across which the atomic bonds are less strong than those parallel to the cleavage directions. By taking advantage of weakness, a large stone can be separated into pieces of more workable size, or a flaw which would mar the finished stone can be eliminated.

When it is decided to cleave a stone, the direction is marked in India ink and a *kerf* or

groove is cut along it with another diamond. The diamond is set on a rigid support and a blunt-edged knife is placed in the kerf. When the back of the knife is tapped with an iron rod, the diamond separates into two pieces. The large thin flat diamonds seen in Indian jewelry may well be cleavage pieces or have been polished from flat triangular or star-shaped twin crystals called *macles*.

Cleavage is seldom used except on large stones, as sawing is found more useful and economically sounder. The sawing machine consists of a frame holding a counterbalanced arm at the end of which the diamond to be sawn is held. Below is a rapidly spinning saw, a thin toothless copper disk whose edge is charged with diamond powder and olive oil. The diamond, nicked with a kerf to start the saw-cut, is lowered on to the saw. This process is slow and it may well take half a day to cut through a one-carat crystal.

If an octahedral crystal is sawn through the center, two four-sided pyramids result, an excellent shape for producing a brilliant-cut stone. But the section is square when a round shape is needed. This is introduced by bruting or grinding, which used to be carried out by rubbing two diamonds together manually. Now one diamond is fixed in a chuck of a motor-driven lathe and ground to shape with another diamond. This gives two stones each shaped like a truncated double cone.

The diamond cutter then polishes facets on this double cone, using a horizontally rotating iron disk called a *scaife*, the surface of which is charged with diamond powder and olive oil. The diamond to be polished is mounted in a holder called a *dop* which can be a cup with a thick copper stem filled with semi-molten solder in which the diamond is set while being polished. A mechanical dop is now more often used with the diamond gripped in claws. The stem of the dop is held in a *tang*, a two-footed wood or metal bridge, so the dop forms the third leg of a tripod. The two feet rest on the mill or workbench and the diamond in the dop rests on the rotating scaife. The position of the dop is adjusted to polish the various facets.

The first facets to be polished are the table and 8 side facets on the crown and a similar set on the pavilion, plus the culet if needed. This is the responsibility of a diamond cutter called a *cross-worker*, on whose skill depend the correct angles which produce the stone's best brilliancy and fire. This partly finished stone then goes to a worker called a *bruter*, who gives it a circular outline. The remaining facets are then put on by the *brillianteerer*, also with a scaife.

The completed stone is then cleaned, examined, weighed and valued. The diamond cutter works by eye and only uses a gauge to check the angles of the pavilion and crown, the latter sometimes

called *bezel* facets. If these angles are wrong—sometimes the shape of the crystal prevents their being adhered to—the *make*, a term used to describe the perfection of cutting, will be wrong. A badly made stone may be too shallow, giving a so-called *laxy* stone that has a fish-eye effect. If too deep, it will produce a lumpy stone which appears to have a dark center.

Commercially, a faceted diamond is graded by its color, clarity, cut and carat weight. These are known as the four C's. Grading is the expert's province, particularly grading for color, as it deals with hardly perceptible differences. Some instrumentation of this work is now possible, using a standard light and a set of previously graded diamonds for comparison, or with electronic apparatus, but these have not been found wholly successful.

The well-known term blue-white for the best colored diamonds is now less acceptable, as these stones may owe their color to a fluorescence induced by ultra-violet rays in daylight. These fluorescent stones are now called *over-blues*. The color grading of diamonds here refers only to white diamonds and does not include stones of a definite color, such as canary yellow, blue, green, pink, red, brown or even black. These are called fancy-colored diamonds, and are sometimes as valuable as fine white diamonds.

The clarity of a diamond depends on the absence of flaws or spots. In commerce a clean diamond is one which shows no blemishes when examined by a corrected lens magnifying 10 times. The cut or make of a diamond refers to the proportions of the stone and the perfection of the cutting. Lastly, the weight needs to be taken into account, for usually the larger the stone, the more valuable it is. The unit of weight for gemstones is the metric carat, which is $\frac{1}{5}$ gram.

The four C's together form the basis of the evaluation of a diamond. A well made flawless stone of fine white color weighing several carats is rare and not readily obtained. Even fine-

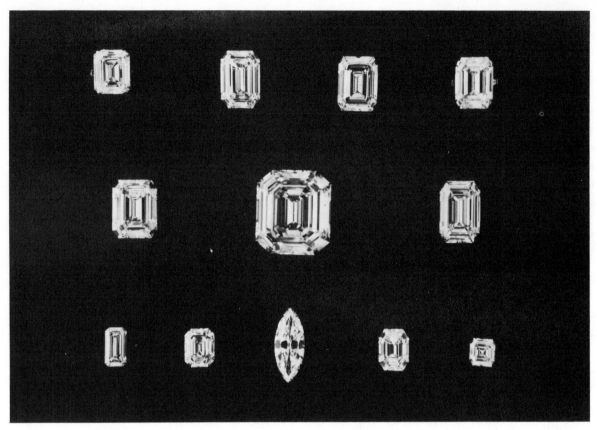

After 12 cuts had been made from the 726-carat Jonker (found on a farm in 1934), the central stone still weighed 142.90 carats.

quality stones weighing a carat or less are scarce and fetch high prices. But stones of slightly lower quality may be just as suitable in jewelry and even, provided they show no glaring blemishes and have no decided tinge of color, be a better buy.

While I do not intend to delve into scientific details, I must mention the effects shown by diamonds under a beam of ultra-violet light. If a woman wearing diamonds visits a laboratory, theater or dance hall where ultra-violet light effects are shown, she may notice that her diamond jewelry glows with varying intensity and even different colors. She may then suspect that not all the stones are diamonds, and be understandably perturbed. She need not worry

for her diamonds are notorious for the inconsistent way they glow.

So-called atomic diamonds are green, yellow, or blue diamonds, which owe their color to bombardment by atomic particles. The so-called off-colored diamonds of the Cape series are the stones usually treated by bombardment. As early as 1904, Sir William Crookes found that he could turn diamonds green by bombarding them with particles emitted from radium compounds. The snag was that the stones then became radio-active. Though scarcely strong enough to be harmful, this radio-activity made detection easy. Few such stones are now known.

After World War II it was found that diamonds could be colored by bombarding

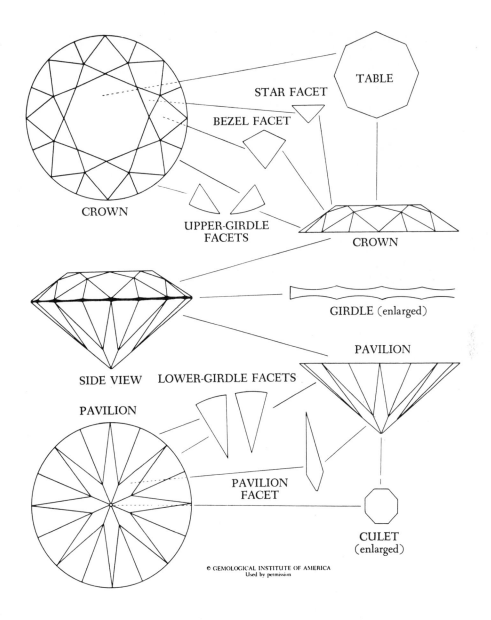

TABLE

STAR FACET

BEZEL FACET

CROWN

UPPER-GIRDLE
FACETS

CROWN

GIRDLE (enlarged)

PAVILION

SIDE VIEW   LOWER-GIRDLE FACETS

PAVILION

PAVILION
FACET

CULET
(enlarged)

them with high-speed particles shot from a cyclotron, or by neutrons from an atomic reactor. Suitable treatment gave a green color, but subsequent heat-treatment turned these greened diamonds to a beautiful yellow. It takes a scientific expert to detect these bombarded diamonds.

It was later found that high-speed electrons could induce a pale greenish-blue color in diamonds similar to the color of natural blue diamonds. But natural blue diamonds are of a special kind, which the scientists call Type 2b. Unlike other diamonds, they conduct electricity. Testing for this needs experience, so it is best left to a trained man.

Only a small percentage of the diamonds mined are suitable for gems. Most of them are only fit for industrial uses. Diamond powder, also known as diamond *grit*, is of great importance in industry. It is made in different

About 2,500 diamond stones pave the surface of the core drill crown produced for Project Mohole, the undersea drilling operation which is to attempt to take cores for study from deeper in the earth's crust than has ever been reached before. The 9-inch diameter crown, which will cut a 3¼-inch core, contains 786 carats of diamond drill material. The unpaved areas of the crown are water channels.

grades and also bonded in metal and plastic work heads used for finishing processes. Diamond has many uses in industry, of which I will mention but a few. Glass-cutting diamonds are well known, but quite large brown and black diamonds are used as turning tools in lathe work in metals and plastics. They produce a superb finish. Electric light-bulb filaments are drawn through diamond wire-drawing dies, and diamonds are used for dressing grinding wheels and as indenters in hardness testing. Styluses for record players are also made of this versatile material.

Diamonds have probably been used in rock drills ever since the Mont Cenis tunnel was cut through the Alps in 1893. A special type of diamond formation is often used in these drills, an aggregate of micro-crystalline diamond and carbon, called carbonado or simply carbon, which forms a compact mass that does not readily break up with use.

Synthetics and Simulants

Many experiments have aimed at synthesizing diamond, but most have been failures and some even fraudulent. The first authentic synthetic diamonds were produced in the early 1950s in Sweden and the United States. High temperature and great pressure were used on a carbonaceous compound. The diamonds that resulted were only of grain size, so had no value as gems but they did have industrial uses. Powder-sized synthetic diamonds are now produced also in South Africa, Ireland, Switzerland, Russia, Japan, and other countries.

The engineering problems involved in building machinery which will withstand the high pressures and high temperatures needed to synthesize diamond prevented the growth of crystals above grit size. But during 1970, by an undisclosed method, the General Electric Company grew diamond crystals of gem quality and as much as a carat in weight. So far the cost of producing them is much greater than that of mining the stones.

The great value and beauty of diamonds leads to their imitation. Many natural and artificial products are available which bear some resemblance to diamond. Before telling the story of these stones, I must mention how some diamonds can be treated to improve them. One trick used to deceive gullible people is to paint a film of blue or violet dye on the rear facets of a yellowish off-colored diamond. The film is so thin it is not noticed, but being the complementary color to yellow, the blue makes the diamond appear whiter. Washing usually removes the dye, but not always, since sometimes a special technique is used that gives more permanent results. Occasionally the diamond doublet is encountered—a composite stone formed of a crown of real diamond and a pavilion of any less valuable colorless stone. The shadow of the table facet on the cement layer joining the two pieces will identify the fake.

The first good imitation of diamond was a faceted special lead glass, called *strass*, a name whose origin is uncertain. Beautifully lustrous and fiery, these stones are convincing imitations but too soft to wear well. They tend to turn brownish, as the sulphide fumes in the air react with the lead in the glass.

Any colorless stones could be said to imitate diamond. Even colorless quartz or rock crystal has been miscalled by such fancy names as Bristol diamond. White topaz is another bright stone, but like quartz lacks fire. Synthetic white sapphire once masqueraded under the misnomer "synthetic diamond," as has synthetic white spinel. Both of these stones have been, and still are, used as imitation diamonds in cheaper lines of jewelry. When small brilliant-cut and baguette-cut stones are used, they may not be easy to detect.

At the turn of the century the best known diamond imitation was white zircon, which went under the name jargoon. This stone has held its own for many years. In recent years a number of newer stones have come from the chemist's laboratory. Several make good diamond simulants, of which three are worth mentioning: strontium titanate, yttrium aluminate, commonly called YAG, and lithium niobate.

Strontium titanate, sold as Fabulite and Diagem, is possibly the more convincing diamond simulant, despite its unusual degree of fire and its low hardness. A later contender, yttrium aluminate, has a garnet type of atomic structure and was earlier called yttrium aluminum garnet, hence YAG. It is harder and has less fire than Fabulite and is sold under the trade names Diamonair and Cirolite. Lithium niobate, sold as Linobate, has much more fire than diamond and about the same hardness as Fabulite, which is very soft compared with diamond.

The layman often asks how a jeweler tells whether a stone is a diamond or not. Briefly, from constantly handling diamonds in his trade, a jeweler gets to know them well and only has doubts in exceptional cases when the stone is somewhat unusual or is badly made. If he knows what to look for, a layman, using a simple hand lens, can see to some extent whether a stone is a diamond or not. But he must know how to use a lens correctly. It should be held close to the eye. If loose, the stone should be held in tongs. If in a setting, hold it in the hand, which should be kept in contact with the hand holding the lens. This keeps the lens steady and allows slight alterations of focus to be made.

Look for any doubling of the rear facet edges. If clearly seen, these prove the stone is not a diamond, but probably a zircon or less likely a lithium niobate. Glass stones and strontium titanate usually show a molded look to the facet edges, which are sharp in diamond. Strontium titanate shows far too much fire, while synthetic sapphires, spinels and YAGs show less fire than diamond. Glass feels warm when touched with the tip of the tongue, while all crystalline stones feel cold. Another good test for diamond is to examine the reflections from the table facet. In diamond the reflections are sharp and undistorted but in other stones the images are slightly blurred.

All gems are graded for color before they are sold because it makes a big difference in price. This grader is checking diamonds for whiteness in a north light in Hatton Garden.

In Thailand (formerly Siam) and Cambodia, rubies and sapphires are mined by families digging small holes to the gravels containing precious stones about 20 feet (6 meters) below the surface. Here on the Thai/Cambodian border a ruby miner descends to fill his bucket which will be winched to the surface by his wife.

3. Ruby and Sapphire

THE SPLENDID RED RUBY and the beautiful blue sapphire seem to have so little in common that it is hard to realize that they are the same mineral, corundum. The derivation of the word corundum is uncertain. It may be an anglicized version of the Tamil *kurundum*, or from the Sanskrit word *korund*. The other two names are easier to account for. Ruby comes from the Latin *rubeus*, meaning red, sapphire from the Greek *sappheiros*, a name for a blue stone.

Pure corundum is colorless. This is the so-called white sapphire. Natural or synthetic stones are only used when an inexpensive imitation diamond is needed. Corundum is a crystallized oxide of aluminum. When it contains a trace of chromium oxide, the crystal turns a glorious red and we have a ruby. If the impurities are iron and titanium, a blue sapphire is produced. Other oxides give corundum other colors—iron oxide gives a green or yellow stone, for example.

Purple and violet sapphires are just a mixture of ruby and sapphire colorings. Pink sapphires are colored with less chromium than it takes to make a ruby, or the chromium is mixed with another metallic oxide. These are border-line cases and the jeweler has to make up his own mind whether to call a stone a ruby, a pink sapphire, or a purple sapphire. Some rubies and sapphires, including a bronze-colored stone, will show a six-pointed star of light when cut as cabochons—that is, with a domed surface. These are star stones. Blue sapphires are always called just sapphires, but those of other colors are prefixed with the color and are collectively known as fancy sapphires.

Rubies

A fair-sized ruby of good color is worth a king's ransom and much more valuable than a diamond of similar size and quality. But the price of ruby and the cheaper sapphires falls more rapidly than the price of diamond with loss of quality, color and size. The dazzling red of Burmese rubies makes them priceless, for those from Thailand (Siam) and certain deposits in Tanzania are tinged brown or violet, which makes them less attractive and less valuable.

The Burmese rubies are found in an area known as the Stone Tract around Mogok in northern Burma. The origin of the mines is unknown but we know they are of great age from the legends which have come down and from the ancient tools found in the workings. The period from the 17th century until the last decades of the 19th century was harsh for the native miners, who worked in intolerable conditions and were heavily taxed by the Burmese kings and their governors.

After the British annexed northern Burma in 1886, the mines were worked by the Burma Ruby Mines Ltd., operating under a concession from the British Government. For some 20 years the company operated the mines successfully by open-cast methods, using machinery. Then came the inception of the synthetic ruby. The company went into liquidation in 1926 and surrendered its lease to the Government in 1931.

Since then the deposits have been worked by native miners, who dig pits called *twinlons* through the overburden to the brownish-yellow ruby-bearing sandy clay called *byon*. When dug out, the byon is washed in shallow baskets and

(Left) In some areas of Sri Lanka (Ceylon) there are gravels about 30 feet (9 meters) below the surface containing ruby, sapphire, garnet, topaz, zircon, tourmaline, spinel and many other gems except diamond. They are mined by making shored pits and winching up gravel baskets filled by men below. (Right) The sandy gravel is washed and swilled in these baskets to remove the sand and lighter elements so that the precious stones, which are generally heavier, remain and can be picked out.

the concentrate of heavy minerals searched by hand for rubies and sapphires. Fine blue sapphires are found in the Stone Tract too, but are more plentiful farther north around Kathe.

Poor quality rubies are found in the vicinity of Madras and Mysore in southern India, some of them showing a star effect. These Indian stones are cut by local lapidaries. Sapphire is found in America and some ruby is found in Macon County, North Carolina, as well as a more abundant deposit at Cowee Creek Valley, where small tabular red and blue crystals are found in alluvial deposits about 2 feet (60 cm) below the

surface. Some of these areas are now opened to the public for a fee.

Small ruby and sapphire crystals have long been known in the Somabula Forest in Rhodesia. Similar crystals have been found in southern Africa, probably in Great Namaqualand, South-West Africa (Namibia). During 1952 a deposit of large opaque ruby crystals up to 6 or 7 in. (15 to 17.5 cm) across was found embedded in bright green black-speckled rock, in Tanzania. These crystals, found at Longido not far from Mount Kilimanjaro, are normally useless for gems, though one enterprising merchant did

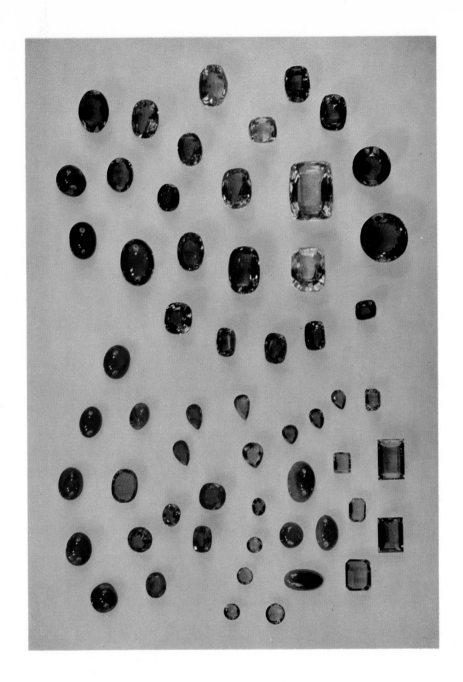

The stones at the top are corundum, universally known as sapphire. The red form of corundum is given a different name, ruby, although the same material. Some rubies are shown at the bottom on the left. The green stones at the bottom on the right are emeralds.

The three stones on the top left edge are all aquamarines and the eight stones at top right all tourmalines. The four stones at bottom left are all zircons—white, brown, blue and green. To the right of them is a chrysoberyl and the three on the right edge at the bottom are green beryl, pink beryl, and golden beryl.

The top seven stones are all garnets, the middle top one being an almandite. The three in the second row are hessonite, rhodolite, and spessartite, and the cabochon stone on the left is a star garnet. The two stones in the middle are green moonstone and orthoclase. Those below are (top row) iolite, sphene, peridot, and white topaz; (middle row) fire opal and topaz; (bottom row) tanzanite, sinhalite, peridot, and blue topaz.

The two top stones to the left are kunzite and next to them are two alexandrites, then two yellow chrysoberyls and two indicolites at the top right. On the left, halfway up, is a cat's-eye and to the right of it, a little higher, a spodumene. The four stones of graduated size in a diagonal row are hiddenites. Bottom left are three sunstones cut en cabochon. The rest of the stones, the smaller ones in the lower half of the picture, are all spinels.

break up the crystals with heat and cut stones from the clearer pieces. The green rock containing the bright red rubies is usually cut and polished for use as an ornamental stone marketed as anyolite, from the Masai word for green.

Ruby and sapphire are both mined along the border of Thailand and Cambodia. The best sapphires are found at Pailin on the Cambodian side. The Thai miners use similar techniques to the Burmese ones. Some of the best sapphires come from this area, but the rubies, better known as Siamese rubies, usually have a distinct brownish-red to violet-red color and are less valued than the fine Burmese stones.

Sapphires

An abundance of sapphires of all colors, but few rubies, are produced in Ceylon (Sri Lanka). These rubies are pale in color, so one does not know whether to call them rubies or pink sapphires. Mining for gems in Ceylon, which produces pebbles of many gem minerals besides sapphires, is carried out much as in Burma, by shallow pit-mining from the alluvial gravel of dried-up river beds. This gravel is called *illam* and is concentrated by panning, using wicker baskets. The concentrate comprising the heavy minerals and gemstones is known as *dullam*. Sapphires from Ceylon are usually pale in color. Though some good blue stones are found, they do not reach the quality of sapphires from Burma and Thailand. Ceylon excels in lovely yellow sapphires and violet, green, brown and colorless stones are also found.

What are said to be the finest sapphires come from the Himalayan district of Kashmir. They were found in 1880 after a landslide had uncovered the deposit in a remote part of the Zaskar Mountains. Situated 15,000 feet (4,500 meters) up, these deposits at first consisted of easily worked friable ground. This petered out and mining later had to penetrate hard rock to find the lenticles (lens-shaped pieces) of feldspar

containing the sapphires, "as thick as plums in a pudding," as one writer put it. In 1956, the area was said to be worked out, but there are probably many more lenticles to be found in this inhospitable mountainous country. Kashmir sapphires are a fine cornflower blue with a beautiful soft velvet luster, due to the very fine inclusions in the stones. This also gives the stones a slight milky mistiness. But not all Kashmir sapphires are superb. Their quality can vary greatly.

The most important North American source of sapphire is the gravels of the Missouri River in Montana, where small rounded light blue, green, pale red and purplish crystals are found. Montana sapphires tend to have a bright metallic luster and, though never large, can be cut into bright attractive stones. Another important American source is Yogo Gulch in Judith Basin County, Montana. This deposit has been worked mechanically, but a cloudburst in 1923 destroyed the plant and the mines were not re-opened until the 1950s. The crystals now recovered are cut in the United States or sent for cutting to Germany or Thailand.

About 1960, sapphire crystals were discovered in the hills along the Umba River in Tanzania. The short prismatic hexagonal crystals are an excellent blue but marred by their yellow core, which prevents stones of any size being cut from them. Sapphires of many shades and also large rubies of a peculiar color very near that of Siamese rubies have emanated from around Morogoro farther south. Similar colored sapphires have since been found in Malawi, formerly Nyasaland. First operated by a British consortium, the mining here has since been taken over by the Malawi government. A source of good quality rubies was found recently by an American geologist in the Tsavo National Park in Kenya. The mine is now owned by the Kenya government. Pakistan is another new supplier of good rubies. There are many other sources of ruby and sapphire across the world, but most provide only impure crystals, unfit for gems. The poor quality ruby with a star effect, which is found in Finland, deserves special mention, however.

We cannot ignore the Australian sapphire deposits either, as they play an important role in the world market today. There are two main locations—the Inverell district in New South Wales and an area around Anakie in Queensland, where the main mining centers are Ruby Vale, Willows and Sapphire. Two types of mining are practiced. *Surfacing*, where the gem-bearing earth is less than 2 feet (60 cm) beneath the surface, simply involves removing and washing it to concentrate the minerals. The gems are then picked out by hand. When the gem gravel or wash is up to 5 feet (1.5 metres) deep, the overburden is first removed with pick and shovel. This is the *stripping* method.

When the "pay dirt" is deep down, shafts are sunk and the gravel is brought up in baskets for screening. It is then washed and searched for gems in the same way. Australian blue sapphires tend to be dark in color and may even be inky black, but the yellow and green stones are often magnificent. A black sapphire with a star effect is also found in Australia.

Star Effects

I have mentioned the star effect several times. Now let me describe it. If a certain type of sapphire or ruby is cut with a dome-shaped surface, called a cabochon cut, it will show three bands of light traveling across the stone. These rays, at an angle of 60° to each other, cross at the apex of the stone and produce a six-pointed star of light. The reason for this is that such crystals are traversed internally by three sets of very fine canals or needles, which run parallel to the sides of the hexagonal prism or pyramid. As they are so fine, light reflected from each of these sets of canals produces a sharp ray of light, like the broader band of light seen crossing the coarser fibers of a reel of silk at right angles.

When there are only patches of intersecting needles in a sapphire, the shimmering flash of light they produce is aptly called "silk." For the best star effect, the stone must be cut in the correct direction, with the top of the stone pointing along the length of the crystal, and viewed by a single overhead light. The stone should not be cut too steep or too flat. The latter gives broad rays which detract from the stone's beauty, as in the native cut golden-brown star stones which have a rather flat dome.

Types of Cut

The most common cut used for colored stones, apart from the cabochon cut just described, is the mixed cut, with a brilliant-cut crown and a trap-cut base or pavilion, though many fine sapphires are now cut in the trap-cut style. Faceting and polishing rubies and sapphires differs from polishing diamonds, which are cut and polished on a single lap (disk). Two separate operations are necessary for ruby, sapphire and all stones other than diamond. The lapidary must first examine the stone to see how best to cut the crystal, for he has to bear in mind certain factors that do not concern the diamond cutter.

Many colored stones, including ruby and sapphire, break up a ray of light into two rays, a phenomenon known as *double refraction*. Each of these rays may show a different color. Scientists call this effect *pleochroism*. It is caused by the two rays absorbing colors differently.

In ruby and sapphire, the best color is seen down the length of the crystal, so the table facet needs to be cut at right angles to this axis. Another factor to be considered, especially with sapphires, is that the color may be patchy. The patch of good color needs to be placed at the base of the stone, so that, by reflection, it appears to fill the stone with color.

Once it is decided where the table facet is to

Some sapphires when cut in a certain direction show a star of reflected light that moves as the stone is moved.

be placed, a large stone is sawn by holding the crystal manually against the edge of a diamond-charged slitting disk. The sawn surface usually forms the table of the stone. Next the stone is ground to shape, complete with facets, on a horizontal lap turned by a hand-driven crank. For sapphire, the lap is charged with diamond powder but less expensive abrasives are used for softer stones. To prepare the stone for cutting, it is cemented onto the end of a gem-stick, which is like an over-sized penholder. The facets are ground on by holding the gem-peg in the hand and pressing it against the surface of the lap. A wooden post partially drilled with a number of small holes, called a jamb-peg, is mounted vertically at the side of the mill or working bench. The end of the gem-stick can be set into the holes in the jamb-peg to give the correct angles for the side facets of the stone.

At this stage the stone is correctly shaped with all its facets but the surfaces have a ground-glass finish. This partially finished stone then goes to the polisher, who polishes the facets put on by the cutter to produce the sparkling surfaces seen in the gems mounted in jewelry. He uses various types of lap—leather-covered, wood and tin, among others—and softer polishing powders such as tripoli powder and chromium oxide, known as green rouge. The stone is then cleaned and weighed.

Simulants

At the turn of the century, the only imitation rubies and sapphires were suitably colored glasses, usually called *pastes*, and garnet-topped doublets, composites made of a red garnet crown fused to a base of suitably colored glass. The colored glass controls the color of the stone,

35

while the garnet top has little influence. These doublets were presumably made to produce a better wearing stone and are occasionally met with today. Glass rubies and sapphires are easily detected by the rolled edges of their facets and the shell-like chips often seen around the edge of the stone. These are best seen with a lens. Garnet-topped doublets show a difference in luster between the garnet and the glass base. Further, the join is rarely symmetrical, so it may be apparent at different distances up the side facets.

Recently some doublets have appeared constructed with the top (crown) of the stone made of a piece of greenish-yellow natural sapphire which is cemented to a base (pavilion) of either synthetic blue sapphire or synthetic ruby to produce simulants of blue sapphire and ruby respectively. As these objects have natural sapphire tops, which usually show natural color banding and "silk" (silky luster) the stones may be readily mistaken for a real stone, especially when the stone is mounted in a setting.

By 1904, the scene had changed. The French scientist A. Verneuil had by then perfected a method of growing ruby and sapphire crystals. This provided a new problem. Detecting these synthetic stones, about which I shall say more later, is not always easy. Sometimes, curved bands of color, fine in ruby and broad in sapphire, and gas bubbles (indicating the stone is man-made) can be seen with a lens. Failing this, a microscope or other technique may be needed. Sometimes sapphires, even if set, can be immersed in oil. When the stone is turned in some direction the curved bands, and even the angular color breaks which indicate a natural stone, will be plainly seen. There is also a blue synthetic spinel made to imitate blue sapphire. It is easily identified, as the glowing image of an electric light bulb viewed through the stone shows a pronounced red edge on one side and blue on the other. The only other stone which produces this effect is a blue paste (glass).

Gem carving is a highly skilled art, especially carving the harder gems like sapphire. This black star sapphire of 1,100 carats (a carat is a fifth of a gram) was carved in the USA and is called "Madonna of the Star."

A number of natural gemstones can resemble ruby and sapphire. The only important ruby simulants are red spinel, garnet, red tourmaline and perhaps an exceptionally red topaz or a rare red zircon. Those resembling sapphire are blue zoisite, spinel, tourmaline and iolite. If you examine a suspect stone under a lens and the rear facet edges are clearly doubled in some directions, the stone may be a tourmaline or a zircon. If, as the stone is turned, the color changes from blue to pale brown or it becomes colorless, then a blue zoisite or iolite is indicated.

This pleochroic effect is much less apparent in other stones even if, as has been suggested, the stone is turned while being viewed through a pair of polaroid spectacles. There are too many variables, but it can be said that if there is a distinct color change, the stone cannot be a spinel, garnet or glass, or a doublet. That is as far as one can go with that idea.

4. Emerald, Aquamarine and the Beryls

THE FINEST COLOR of the beautiful emerald is a rich velvety green, though all shades from a very pale to an over-saturated green are met with in cut stones. Emerald is the prized member of the beryl family of minerals. Its sisters are the well-known sea-green to blue aquamarine, the pink-colored beryl called morganite, and the yellow-colored beryls, the more deeply tinted of which are sometimes called heliodor, a name which means "a gift from the sun." There are green beryls, too, which are not emeralds for reasons I will explain later. Many other beryls are colorless or nearly so, and have little importance in jewelry.

Held in high esteem by the ancients, the emerald is the symbol of faith and is said to be a balm to tired eyes. Tradition makes this stone the symbol of success. The finest emeralds transcend the diamond in value, but their worth decreases much more sharply than that of diamond with size and color. Emeralds are notoriously flawed, too often very much so, and a large perfectly clean emerald of excellent color is rare.

The earliest source of emeralds was the so-called Cleopatra's mines of Upper Egypt, which lie in a range of mountains running parallel to the west coast of the Red Sea. Lost for centuries, these mines were rediscovered by the Frenchman F. Cailliaud. This dispelled the notion that the emeralds of ancient times reached the Middle East from America via the Orient. These Egyptian mines produced only inferior stones and are not worked now.

The most beautiful emeralds are found in South America. The mines were known to the natives before the Spanish invasion. The Spaniards seized many fine emeralds among the treasures they found and carried them away, but did not find the actual workings until 1558. These lie some 75 miles (110 km) north-west of Bogatá, the capital of Colombia. There are several mines in the area, the most important being Muzo, El Chivor, Cosquez and Gachala.

The high quality of Colombian emeralds is probably due to the fact that the crystals are found in bituminous limestone, whereas the host rock in all the other sources is a mica schist. Emeralds are mined by cutting steps in the mountain side and recovering the emeralds from pockets. The remaining debris is washed down the mountain side by rushes of water released from reservoirs situated higher up. *Canutillos* is the name given to the good crystals suitable for fashioning into gemstones. The ill-formed inferior crystals are called *morallons*. An interesting type of emerald from this locality is known as a trapiche emerald, whose crystals have a core and spokes of dark brown or black beryl with green beryl filling the interstices between them. Stones are cut from the green sections, but they have an unnatural misty translucent appearance.

During 1830 emerald was found near Sverdlovsk (formerly Ekaterinburg) in Russia. The mines are on the Asian side of the Ural Mountains. Though large crystals were often found, their quality was poor and only the smaller ones reached anything like the quality of the South American stones. As far as is known, mining there now is only sporadic.

In Colombia, emeralds are mined by cutting terraces into the side of gem-bearing mountains, thus exposing pockets containing the precious green stones.

It was not until 1927 that emeralds were found in Africa in the Leysdorp area of the Transvaal. They contain extensive flaws and are usually marred by flakes of mica, which give them a brownish tinge, so they can never become quality stones. The bulk of them used to be sold to Indian merchants for cutting and mounting into jewelry, but since *apartheid* became a world issue, the direct supply to India seems to have stopped.

Mainly as a result of the wartime search for strategic minerals mica and beryl, emeralds were found in the Kaliguman area of Udaipur, India during 1943. These Indian emeralds are equal in many respects to the Siberian stones, which had earlier been sent to Jaipur in India. During later years more deposits were found around Udaipur and also in the Ajmere-Merwara district. These Indian crystals are found in a mica schist, but their quality varies greatly and few stones are of first-class quality. Most are suitable only for low-priced jewelry or fashioning into beads.

Emeralds from Brazil are said to have been known since the 16th century, but their early history is unreliable. It is only since the last century that they have been extensively marketed. Most of them are a pale yellowish-green and usually clear, so much so that they are often not accepted as emeralds. The deposits lie in the states of Minas Gerais, Bahia and Goias.

During the latter half of the 1950s, small but fine quality emeralds were discovered near Belingwe in the southern part of Rhodesia. They are called Sandwana emeralds, from the name of the small valley where the discoverers first made camp. The crystals, small hexagonal prisms common to beryl, are now of some importance in gem commerce. Other deposits have been found in this vicinity recently.

Since the 1960s, emeralds of fair quality have come from the Chitral district of Pakistan and have entered commerce in European countries. The old source of emerald at Habachtal in Austria and that at Emmaville in New South Wales are not commercially attractive, but the find at Cue in Western Australia has recently been reported active. Miku in Zambia and northern Mozambique are other modern sources not yet fully exploited.

A special filter, known as the Chelsea color filter, has been made as a test for emeralds. It is so constructed that it passes a band of deep red light and a band of yellow-green light. Emeralds as a rule pass deep red but not yellow-green, so they appear red through the filter. Imitation emeralds show green. This filter is now less efficient, for some modern emeralds do not show the residual red color, neither do some of the newer synthetic emeralds.

Robert Webster, FGA, author of this book, is an internationally famed gemmologist. He has carried out much research at the London Gem Laboratory, where he is seen in the picture here looking at a stone through a Chelsea filter.

The green color in emerald is caused by a trace of chromium, the same element which gives ruby its red color. There are other green beryls, most of which owe their color to iron and are a duller green. Some stones from the Salininha mine in Bahia, Brazil, and from a mine in Pakistan are not colored by chromium, but possibly by its sister element, vanadium. Scientifically they should not be called emeralds, though they have a fair emerald color, often better than that of some poor quality emeralds. The problem is whether to consider science or beauty the more important. The buyer of emerald jewelry need have little fear, for such vanadium-colored stones are few and far between.

Like all other gemstones, apart from diamond, emerald is fashioned by the same methods used for ruby and sapphire. The crystal is sawn, the facets ground on and then separately polished on another lap. Most emeralds are shaped in the trap-cut style with cut corners to give the so-

called emerald cut. The mixed-cut is rarely used for emeralds but badly flawed stones are cut as cabochons or beads. Even small figurines have been carved from large flawed crystals.

Emerald Simulants

Emerald is such an important stone that I must mention some of its simulants before describing the other varieties of beryl. First of them and the most important is the synthetic emerald. The present successful syntheses stem from the attempt by J. J. Ebelmen, one-time Director of the Sèvres porcelain factory in France, to grow commercially viable emerald crystals in the laboratory.

But it was not until 1947 that a truly successful commercial synthetic emerald was produced. This was the work of Carroll F. Chatham of San Francisco. These Chatham-created emeralds, as they are called in the United States, held the market until 1964, when the French firm of

One of the most treasured gems is emerald, which is rare and only very occasionally found without natural inclusions inside it, in which case it is extremely costly. The central emerald in this brooch weighs over 72 carats.

Pierre Gilson and the German Zerfass firm produced their commercial products, later followed by the Linde firm's product, which resulted from a different technique. A Canadian firm is also now producing synthetic emerald. The different methods used to grow synthetic emeralds will be described in a later chapter.

Another type of emerald simulant is the emerald-coated beryl. First called Emerita and now Symerald, it was first produced in Austria. The stones are made by depositing a layer of synthetic emerald on a preformed beryl of pale color. The faces are then lightly polished.

No tell-tale curved structure lines or gas bubbles can be seen in synthetic emeralds as in synthetic rubies and sapphires. The visible features look very natural as they are grown in much the same way as natural stones. Consequently, to be sure of emeralds one must have recourse to an experienced jeweler or a gem laboratory.

Apart from garnet-topped doublets with a green glass base, and imitation stones made of green glass, the only other stones made to imitate emerald are the so-called soudé emeralds, of which there are several kinds. The earliest of these composite stones consisted of two pieces of rock crystal, forming the top and base of the stone, cemented together with green gelatine, or later a more permanent green material. About 1950, a new type was produced in which the rock crystal was replaced by synthetic white spinel. A more recent innovation uses two pieces of pale aquamarine, or even pale emerald.

Such composite stones are readily identified when unset by being immersed in liquid and examined edge-on. The colorless top and bottom sections are then easily seen with the dark line of the colored layer between them. When the stones are set in jewelry, identification this way is more difficult.

Aquamarine

Aquamarine, unlike emerald, is often found as large clear crystals in pegmatite, a coarse granite rock, from which quite large clear-cut stones can be fashioned. Aquamarine varies in color from sky-blue to bluish-green and takes its name from these, the colors of sea water. The bright sky-blue aquamarines which make such lovely jewels are rarely encountered in nature. They are nearly always the result of heat treatment of greenish and yellowish beryls.

Aquamarine is widespread and found in many places, but the most important deposits are in the Teopilo Otoni district between the Jequitinhona and Doce Rivers of Brazil. Madagascar, Nigeria and the Ural Mountains in Siberia are other sources which deserve mention.

Aquamarines, which are noted for their clarity and freedom from flaws, are usually cut in the trap style. But the mixed-cut is often used, when the stones are mostly cut as drops and long ovals, which suit the long prismatic crystals and allow the table facet to be parallel to the length of the prism, the direction of best color.

The most important simulant of aquamarine is the similar-colored synthetic spinel. These stones can be most deceptive, but often have a slight violet tinge and altogether too bright a luster. Though deceptive to look at, synthetic spinels are the easiest of aquamarine simulants to identify, as they show an orange residual color when viewed through the Chelsea filter, while the true aquamarine shows a strong blue.

A garnet-topped doublet is also made with a light blue base to imitate the aquamarine, but such composite stones are not common. There are many types of glass imitations of aquamarine, many of excellent color and clarity. They can be most deceptive. One is the so-called "mass aqua," an especially hard type of glass. As glass is a bad conductor of heat, pastes (as glass gems are usually called) feel warm to the touch, whereas a genuine stone feels quite cold. For this test to be effective, the stone must be picked up with tongs and not the fingers, and then gently touched with the tip of the tongue. To gain experience, practice this test with a piece of rock crystal and a piece of glass.

Other Beryls

The lovely pink beryl, called morganite, after the banker, J. P. Morgan, is less often seen in Europe than in America, for the main sources of this variety are in California and in Brazil, though large rich rose colored crystals are found in the island of Madagascar. The yellow beryls are also less commonly encountered than aquamarine and less used, for there are so many yellow stones that they do not stand out. They come from Brazil and South-West Africa.

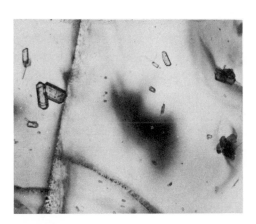

This is what a gemmologist will look for through his microscope if he is testing an emerald to see if it is real. These inclusions indicate that the emerald— although true emerald—was made in a factory in France and is not natural.

5. The Garnets

GARNETS are beautiful stones with a high luster and a strong color and are generally fairly hard and durable. There has always been a prejudice against garnets, for some kinds are comparatively abundant and relatively cheap. For these reasons they used not to be popular with the buying public. It is different today. Probably for the same reasons, many garnets were given all kinds of inaccurate names in earlier days. What is more, many garnets are very nearly the same color as the prized ruby. The layman does not generally appreciate that there is not one garnet, but several different sub-species and varieties, one of which, the green demantoid garnet, is a most valuable stone.

The garnet family supplies an interesting group of gemstones in rich colors. They are now far more highly prized than at any time in their history, even the heyday of Victorian jewelry set with rose-cut pyropes and carbuncles.

Almandite

The most common garnet used in jewelry is almandite, or almandine garnet, which varies in color from blood-red to violet-red. Some of these garnets are so dark in color that, if cut with a normal arrangement of gem facets, they would appear practically black. To overcome this, some dark stones are fashioned in the cabochon style with the back of the stone hollowed out to make them lighter. These are the carbuncles of earlier days.

Almandites of a less intense color are usually cut in the mixed-cut or trap-cut styles, and the rose cut is rarely used. Some of these garnets, particularly those found in America, are polished to an irregular shape called *baroque* by a tumbling process. This is done by mixing the rough pebbles with grinding powder, then with polishing powder, in a churn-like barrel, which is rotated mechanically. The tumbler rolls the pebbles around until they are ground and polished to an irregular shape.

Garnet forms in spherical crystals with 12, 24 or more flat faces. When these crystals are eroded, they look like musket balls, and have even been so used in earlier days. Necklaces of almandite garnets are sometimes encountered, made simply of these round crystals drilled through the center. If brilliant, as they often are, the original crystal faces are left or sometimes lightly polished.

Some faceted almandites can look remarkably like some Thailand (Siam) rubies and it can be difficult to distinguish them by eye alone. A lens examination of these garnets may often show a coarse reticulation (network effect) of crossed needles and sometimes fairly large included crystals. If seen, these identify the stone as garnet. It is a wise precaution to compare inclusions seen in unknown stones with those seen in stones whose species is certain.

Almandite garnets, as jeweler and public know them, belong to a series, as there is a gradation of garnet types between the iron-rich almandite garnet and the magnesium-rich pyrope garnet, which will be discussed later. This series, which does not perturb the jeweler or the buyer, is due to the replacement of one element in the gem's chemical make-up with any amount of another. The scientist calls this effect *isomorphous* replacement.

At Pforzheim, in southern Germany, there are many gem setters. This is a typical jewelers' bench where the men who set gems are at work.

Much almandite comes from Jaipur and some other areas of India. Some of these garnets display a four-rayed star of light when suitably cut, an effect caused by needle-like inclusions, comparable to the oriented needles which cause the star effect in the sapphire. But the star in garnet, though usually sharp, is rather weak and may be seen only with difficulty. Trincomalee on the north-east coast of Ceylon (Sri Lanka) supplies much garnet of this type. Other leading sources are in Tanzania, Zambia, Madagascar, Central and South America, particularly Brazil, but it occurs world wide.

The United States is a prolific supplier of almandite garnets. In Macon County, North Carolina, a rhododendron-red garnet is found to which the name rhodolite has been given. However, much larger rhodolite garnets of similar color are now found in Tanzania, near Beit's Bridge in Rhodesia and in Ceylon. Some star garnet is found at Emerald Creek, Latah County, Idaho.

Pyrope

Pyrope garnet, nearly always blood-red in color, was originally found near Trebnitz in the northeast of the old kingdom of Bohemia, now part of Czechoslovakia. These garnets are small and found weathered out of the rock. The rose-cut garnets so often seen in Victorian jewelry were made from these small crystals. Pyropes of better quality are found in the alluvial and mine concentrates of South African diamond mines. Pyrope garnet is also found in many other places such as Australia, Brazil, Argentina, Mexico and the United States where, particularly in Arizona, pebbles are found in ant hills, thrown out by the ants in their burrowings.

Grossular Garnet

The next type to be discussed is called grossular garnet. Two transparent varieties of this type of garnet are faceted and used in jewelry. Best known of these are the yellowish-red to sunrise-red stones which go under the name hessonite. Hessonites are readily recognized by their resinous or oily look due to peculiar syrupy streaks in the stone and the inclusion of many small bubble-like crystals, both of which can usually be seen with a hand lens. These garnets are fairly hard. They take and retain a fairly good polish and are quite brilliant stones. Comparatively recently a transparent green grossular garnet has entered the gem market. Bright emerald-green to a paler yellowish-green, these stones are found in Pakistan, Tanzania, and Kenya. They have been named Tsavorite.

A massive rock-like grossular garnet should be mentioned, for it yields an ornamental stone which, when green, closely resembles jade. This rock-like stone, usually called massive grossular garnet, or more correctly by scientists, hydrogrossular garnet, was first found in the Transvaal, South Africa. It became known as Transvaal jade or South African jade, but the stone is not jade, so these names are not admissible. The material has a horny texture and breaks, with difficulty, with a splintery fracture. Besides its green form, this stone has also been found in pink, blue or grey, which, like the green, are often cut into cabochons for jewelry. A similar type of massive grossular garnet has recently been obtained from Pakistan, the United States and New Zealand. But much of the material is a mixture of grossular garnet and a related mineral called idocrase.

Another kind of rock, strictly speaking a marble, which is occasionally used for ornamental purposes, consists of pink crystals of grossular garnet embedded in greyish-white marble. Known as xalostocite, it comes from Xalostoc, Morelos in Mexico.

Demantoid Garnet

The most important and valuable garnet is demantoid. Though somewhat softer than other garnets, it produces a magnificent stone varying from greenish-yellow to rich emerald green. Though masked to some extent by the body color, the demantoid garnet has a fire greater than that of diamond itself, and with its high luster, its general appearance is characteristic. Apart from this, close examination of the interior of the stone with a lens may show fine silky fibers of asbestos, which radiate from a single point or look like pony-tails. No other green stone shows similar inclusions, so their presence is conclusive evidence for demantoid garnet.

The name demantoid is derived from the stone's adamantine luster. As the name lacks euphony, jewelers often call these green garnets olivine or olivene. But using these names for green demantoid garnet is open to serious objection, since olivine is the correct name for a mineral which in gem quality is the jeweler's peridot.

True demantoid garnets are found only in the Ural Mountains, which separate European from Asian Russia. They are found as rounded pebbles in an asbestos serpentine, or loose in beds of streams. The finest examples, and demantoid garnets are always small with stones rarely above five carats in weight, are found in the gold washings around Nizhii-Tagil on the

Siberian side of the Urals. In the Ala valley in Piedmont, Italy, and in the Zermatt, Switzerland, small yellowish garnets are found identical, except in color, with the demantoid garnet. Such stones have been called topazolites, but as this name is likely to cause confusion with topaz, it is better to call them yellow demantoid garnets.

Demantoid garnet is a sub-variety of the so-called common garnet, whose mineralogical name is andradite. This garnet is normally black and its sole connection with the jeweler's art is that these black crystals have occasionally been fashioned for use in mourning jewelry.

Spessartite

A rare and attractive garnet is spessartite, named from Spessart in Bavaria where it was first found. In color and appearance it closely resembles hessonite, but usually has a livelier appearance without the oily look of hessonite. Spessartites are prized more by the collector than the jeweler, for they are as yet insufficiently well known to be easily marketed. They are found in Burma, the Ceylon gem gravels, Madagascar, Brazil, and in parts of the United States, notably California.

6. Topaz and Tourmaline

To MOST PEOPLE topaz is a brownish-yellow stone which has been likened to the color of sherry. They may also have heard of pink topaz, but much topaz is colorless and there are also pale blue stones which resemble, but are regretfully overshadowed by, the aquamarine. The colorless stones, called white topaz, are scarcely worth the cost of cutting and rarely seen except as surrounding stones in some older pieces of jewelry.

The name topaz has been used indiscriminately for real topaz and for yellow-colored quartz. The reason for this goes a long way back in history. In early times the name topaz was apparently used for a green stone, probably the gem we now know as peridot. Later, before the chemistry of gem minerals was known, the name was applied to many yellow stones, whatever their exact nature. In the 18th century, when crystals from Schneckenstein, Germany, were first correctly analyzed and identified, the mineralogist concerned named this mineral topaz. This choice of a name known and indiscriminately used for so many centuries was an unhappy one.

Until quite recently the German cutters of Idar-Oberstein always called the yellow quartz they cut into gemstones, and which forms much of their trade, by the name topaz, or by hybrid names like quartz-topaz or topaz-quartz. To the ordinary buyer these hybrid names mean very little. To try and overcome this difficulty, the real topaz is often called precious topaz or Brazilian topaz, for the only source of sherry-brown and pink topazes is the Ouro Preto district of Brazil. But yellow quartz also comes from Brazil, so the position becomes worse

confounded. Using the name topaz for any mineral but the true topaz now comes under the stricture of law in some countries.

Gem topazes fall into two fairly well defined groups with distinctly different physical and optical properties. The sherry-colored and pink stones, prized for jewelry, form one group, and the colorless and pale blue stones the other. This division into groups is of no interest to the layman, but is of some importance to gemmologists in testing such gems.

As already mentioned, the sherry-brown and pink topazes are found only in one locality, Ouro Preto in Brazil. Pink stones are rarely found in nature, but are the result of heat treatment of brown stones. Heating must be gradual, so that the crystals do not crack, and is often carried out by enclosing the stone in many wrappings of tinder, which is then set on fire. Otherwise the stones may be placed in charcoal or some other inert substance and then heated. The temperature necessary is about 450°C. (840°F.) and slow cooling is essential. If a stone is overheated, the result is colorless; if insufficiently heated, it turns salmon-pink rather than the prized rose-pink. The color obtained is permanent.

Blue and colorless stones are found in many parts of the world, particularly Brazil and West Africa, but only the blue stones are important in jewelry, mainly from their similarity to aquamarine. The colorless stones have little value. Much white topaz is found as rolled pebbles, which the uninitiated sometimes think are diamonds. In some West African countries the natives sell rolled pebbles of supposedly blue topaz, which are really of white topaz colored on the outside by dropping them in an indigo dye pot, a conspicuous feature by the roadside in some parts of Africa.

Topaz, which has a slippery feel, shows a more brilliant luster than the quartz gems. What is more important, topaz crystals have a direction of weakness along which they will break fairly easily, leaving a smooth surface. This cleavage, as it is called, may occur in a number of minerals besides diamond, already mentioned. In topaz, this weak direction lies in all planes at right angles to the length of the crystal, and as the crystals are most commonly long and pencil-shaped, stones cut from them are often long–shaped or pear-shaped. These cut stones are very liable to break across if knocked, or at least may be seriously flawed.

Topaz Simulants

The classic imitation of sherry topaz is the brownish-yellow quartz already referred to. Glass imitations are usually obvious on sight. If not, their lack of hardness will give them away, for they will not scratch window glass. Glass is warm to the touch too, while a real stone feels cold, and does not have the slippery feel of topaz. Composite stones of the soudé type, consisting of two pieces of white synthetic spinel with a brown coloring layer between, have been marketed and make good imitation topaz.

A number of other natural stones can resemble the various colors of topaz. Yellow sapphire and golden-yellow chrysoberyl may be close in color to yellow topaz. Pink tourmaline can resemble pink topaz in luster and appearance, but can be distinguished from topaz by the apparent doubling of the rear facet edges when looked through with a lens. Tourmaline shows this effect strongly, while topaz barely does at all. Pink beryl, pink sapphire and pink spinel may also resemble pink topaz, and blue topaz so closely resembles aquamarine that it is not easy to distinguish them from each other on sight.

Tourmaline

The mineral tourmaline probably shows a greater variety of color than any other gem species. The most common color is green, varying from a rather typical dark leaf-green to pale green. Green tourmaline has a certain appeal, stronger in some countries than others, but the tourmaline popular in some other countries is the pink variety known as rubellite. This name is now going out of circulation in favor of the unambiguous name pink tourmaline. Occasionally one meets a rich rose-red tourmaline, which reaches the color of some rubies, and there is a blue, the least common color of tourmaline, called indicolite.

A violet-red stone has a unique appeal owing to its color. As it first came from Siberia, it is known as siberite. Yellow tourmaline make quite attractive stones, but colorless stones, called achroite, are rather insipid and moreover, extremely rare. The more attractive shades of yellowish-brown to very deep brown are fashioned and mounted in jewelry, while black tourmaline, called schorl, possibly the commonest kind of tourmaline, has been cut for mourning jewelry.

In former days, even as late as the Victorian era, various hybrid and misleading names were used for different tourmalines. Green tourmaline was often known as Brazilian emerald. This may well be because, when searching for emerald in the early days in Brazil, miners found a number of green crystals which they thought to be emeralds. When these were sent to Europe, they were found to be tourmalines. Other misnomers were Brazilian sapphire for blue tourmalines and Brazilian peridot for greenish-yellow stones, while tourmalines of honey-yellow color were often called Ceylon chrysolite. In these enlightened times, these names should not be used.

Not all gems are polished in facets or dome shapes (en cabochon) today. The bracelet above by designer Gilian E. Packard is set with slices of a natural crystal of tourmaline set in gold.

The convention today is to use the name tourmaline prefixed with its color.

There is often variation of coloring within a tourmaline crystal. One end of the crystal may be green and the other pink, with sometimes a yellow or colorless band between. Stones are occasionally cut from these parti-colored crystals and make unusual jewel stones. In another type of parti-coloration, the color changes along the length of the crystal. The core may be green, surrounded by white or yellow and have a pink outer layer, or vice-versa. Crystals arranged like this are called watermelon tourmalines. Some tourmalines may be fibrous, containing parallel fibers or canals running through the length of the crystal. Cabochon stones cut from these crystals produce cat's-eyes, but the effect is much

less sharp than cat's-eyes of chrysoberyl or even quartz.

Most tourmaline is fashioned in the mixed-cut style but fine quality tourmalines may be fashioned in the trap-cut style, or a modification of it called the scissors cut. The cat's-eye material is cut out in the cabochon fashion, while material which is badly flawed is fashioned as beads or even carved into small figurines, as such tourmaline crystals can be quite large.

Tourmaline crystals are usually long prisms. Viewed down their length, they show a rounded triangular outline. When they show faces at each end of the prism, they will be seen to vary in steepness at each end, an outward sign of polarity. Indeed, when Dutch traders first brought tourmalines from Ceylon to Europe they called them "ashentrekker," which means dust collector, since when the crystals are warmed and then slowly cooled, they assume an electric charge, positive at one end of the crystal and negative at the other. This is why tourmalines in a jeweler's window, which can get decidedly warm, collect dust more readily than any other gemstone. Tourmaline's polarity is of technological interest, for among other things, an electric charge can be produced by pressure and slices of suitably cut tourmaline are used in depth gauges for submarines.

Gem tourmaline is found in many parts of the world, particularly Brazil, Ceylon and the Pala district of southern California. Much tourmaline in many colors is found in Madagascar and in the Ural Mountains of Russia. South-West Africa is another source of gem crystals, some of which, those from Usakos, for example, are nearly emerald green, while other stones turn an emerald green when heated to a moderate temperature. Some deep red tourmalines are found in the Alto Ligonha district of Mozambique. Tourmaline also comes from Rhodesia and from Tanzania, where a green tourmaline is found which owes its color to traces of vanadium and chromium. These stones show red through the filter, whereas normal green tourmalines do not.

Tourmaline Simulants

The color of deep green tourmalines is usually so typical that it is obvious what they are, but the lighter green stones are more deceptive. The pink stones are so like pink topaz in luster and color that they are not readily distinguishable from each other by eye. It is only when a lens is used to see the rather pronounced doubling of the rear facets that it can be proved the stone is tourmaline, and this takes experience. Green tourmalines are well imitated by synthetic green spinel, but there is no doubling of the facet edges when one looks through this stone. An ordinary glass imitation of tourmaline is usually obvious, but glass "stones" have been seen with a spun-glass structure made up of long drawn-out bubbles. These produce a very convincing cat's-eye tourmaline, which has deceived even experienced jewelers.

7. Chrysoberyl and Moonstone

TWO OF THE more interesting gemstones belong to the group of minerals known as chrysoberyl. Alexandrite is one, the other is the cat's-eye, sometimes known as cymophane. The less common chrysoberyls vary from brown through golden-brown to greenish-yellow, the latter popular in Victorian jewelry, when it was often called chrysolite, a term now little used.

Yellow chrysoberyl, so popular in the 19th century, has such a distinctive color that the stones are easily identified. The only stones that imitate them are the synthetic spinel and similarly colored glass, both characterized by their strong apple-green glow under ultra-violet light, an effect seen even in daylight. Brown chrysoberyls are much harder to identify by mere inspection, but are unimportant as jewels.

Alexandrite

The most important of the chrysoberyls is alexandrite, a most fascinating gemstone owing to its spectacular variation in color according to the type of light it is viewed by. In daylight, which is much richer in blue rays, alexandrite shows a fine green, under artificial light it appears raspberry-red. But do not view this stone under electric fluorescent tube lighting or you will be disappointed since, like daylight, this light contains more blue than red, and the alexandrite will not show its spectacular color change.

The scientific reason for this change in different lights of alexandrite (not the only stone to do so) is that the stone absorbs the orange and yellow-green rays from white light. The eye then picks up a region of red light and another of bluish-green light. Any change in the strength of either color in the incident light will alter their balance and the appearance of the stone.

Alexandrite is named after Alexander II, Russian tsar, as it is said to have first been found on his birthday, 17th April, 1834. The crystals were found at the emerald mines on the Takovara river in the Ural Mountains, some 56 miles from Sverdlovsk, formerly known as Ekaterinburg. It is here that the last tsar, Alexander's grandson, Nicholas II, and his family are said to have been murdered in 1918. Stones cut from Russian crystals are a good bluish-green and show an excellent color change, but they are small and usually contain flaws.

The other major source of alexandrite is the Ceylon gem gravels, where it occurs as rolled pebbles big enough to make fairly large cut stones. Alexandrites from Ceylon usually show a purer green than the bluish-green Russian stones, but the color change is not so good. In artificial light the color is a brownish-red rather than the violet-red shown by stones from the Urals. A few alexandrites have been found in the Mogok Stone Tract of northern Burma, but this source is unimportant. Large, but rather impure alexandrite crystals have been found in Rhodesia but are unimportant as cut stones.

Alexandrites are hard stones and take an excellent polish. Their high luster and intriguing color change make them valuable stones. But there are also green chrysoberyls which show no color change and cannot be called alexandrites. Some other stones show only a slight color change and it is difficult to decide whether to call them alexandrites or green chrysoberyls. Anyway, the better the color change, the more valuable the stone. The mixed-cut style is usually used for alexandrite, as it brings out the color change most effectively, but the trap-cut style is sometimes used.

Alexandrite Simulants

There used not to be any synthetic alexandrites, but they are now being grown as crystals in the United States and marketed commercially as cut stones. While there are many synthetic alexandrites on the market, they are not chrysoberyl, but synthetic fancy-colored corundum, a different species altogether. These synthetic corundums, or synthetic fancy sapphires, are quite cheap and usually fashioned in the cross-cut style, sometimes called the scissors cut. This is a modification of the trap cut, in which each of the side facets is further cut into four triangular facets. Round or oval brilliant-cut stones are fashioned from this synthetic sapphire and set in earrings and fringe necklaces.

When closely compared with true alexandrite, these synthetic alexandrite-type sapphires are seen to be quite different. In daylight they are greyish-green rather than rich green like the real stone, and in artificial light the red is more purplish and resembles some deep-hued amethysts. The fact that most people, and even some jewelers, have rarely, if ever, seen a true alexandrite explains why these synthetic sapphires are not more readily identified. When examined with a hand lens, they usually show quite strongly curved striations, and sometimes gas bubbles, convincing evidence of synthesis.

Another synthetic color-change stone made to imitate alexandrite is a synthetic spinel. It is usually a better imitation of alexandrite than the synthetic sapphire, for the green color in daylight is much more like the real stone's and the red shown in artificial light nearer to that shown by poor quality alexandrites. These stones are seldom met with, probably because they are difficult to grow.

An exceptional and rarely encountered kind of counterfeit alexandrite is a composite stone made on the soudé emerald principle from two pieces of rock crystal cemented together with a suitable colored binder, probably an organic dyestuff in gelatine or some other cementing material. Such a stone can easily be detected if immersed in water, when the clear top and bottom will be seen, separated by the dark line of the colored layer. The color change of this fake is like that shown by the synthetic sapphire simulant. A paste stone made with swirls of two different colors of glass has been made, presumably to imitate alexandrite, but it is obvious and easily detected.

If you think a stone may be an alexandrite, stand it on a black surface or cloth and direct a beam of light from a desk lamp into it. Then view it through one lens of a pair of polaroid spectacles. If the stone is an alexandrite, it will be bright green and change to bright red as the polaroid is turned.

Cat's-Eye

Cat's-eye, the other important member of the chrysoberyl family, owes its fascination to the streak of light which crosses the stone when it is cut in the cabochon style. For the best effect the top domed face should be cut rather steeply, with the back of the stone less steeply domed. The cat's-eye effect is caused by the reflection of light from vast numbers of very fine parallel tubes which run through it. The finer the tubes, the sharper the ray. The ray in chrysoberyl cat's-eyes is usually much sharper than in other stones which show this effect, such as quartz and tourmaline. The cat's-eye effect is, in fact, a simpler version of the effect seen in star stones, with only one set of parallel canals giving just one ray of light, crossing the run of the canals at right angles.

The most highly prized color of chrysoberyl cat's-eyes, most of which come from Ceylon, is honey-yellow, though all shades of yellow,

51

brown and green are met with, including a very rare alexandrite cat's-eye which is extremely valuable. A perfect cat's-eye should be as transparent as the canals allow, and the cat's-eye ray should be straight as well as sharp. Opaque pale yellowish-green chrysoberyl cat's-eyes are more common, but of low value. Some chrysoberyl cat's-eyes are found in Brazil.

Cat's-Eye Simulants

The only important simulant of chrysoberyl cat's-eyes is chatoyant yellow quartz. Fine quality quartz cat's-eyes closely resemble those of chrysoberyl, but the ray is generally more diffuse, owing to the larger size of the tubes. Recently cat's-eyes have appeared in rarer stones like apatite and diopside, as well as the tourmaline cat's-eyes already mentioned, and an occasional cat's-eye emerald or green beryl. A yellow or green synthetic or natural star sapphire cut to show only one arm of the star might appear as a cat's-eye. A few such freaks have been cut from synthetic material in the United States. Cat's-eye pastes are made, from which a chatoyant (cat's-eye) effect is obtained by including parallel tubes of drawn-out bubbles in the glass. These are rather crude and fairly obvious.

I should also mention the so-called cat's-eyes made from dark-colored sea shell. Usually cut as rather flat cabochons, these are generally brown or greenish-brown with a broadish eye that does not exhibit the sharp ray of stone cat's-eyes. One may be puzzled by them at first, but once seen and identified, they are obvious.

Moonstone

Moonstone is the best known gemstone of the feldspar family of minerals. It is a colorless stone with milky overtones, better quality examples of which show a bluish flash of light as they are turned. This effect is due to the interference of light between very thin plates of two different feldspars. For the best effect these plates must lie parallel to the base of the cabochon-cut stone. This style of cutting is the best for moonstones. Moonstones can be seen to good advantage if made into beads composed of two cabochons base to base.

Moonstone, which sometimes shows a cat's-eye effect, comes mainly from Ceylon, though a darker variety is found in Burma. There is a constant demand for this stone, which is used for cheaper jewelry and attractive bead necklaces. Good quality material is now getting scarce, which must eventually boost the stones' value, provided no new sources of supply become available.

Any simulant of moonstone would seem unnecessary, but at least two stones have been made to imitate it. They are a schillerized rock crystal, heat treated to produce a "schiller" or milkiness —and a similarly treated white spinel. But neither truly reproduces the moonstone's lovely blue sheen.

Other Feldspars

An unusual orthoclase feldspar stone, of the group to which moonstone belongs, is a clear transparent yellow variety found in Madagascar. Stones cut from this material are mainly collectors' items and rarely found mounted in jewelry. Microcline feldspar, better known as Amazon-stone, is another of the group, quite often used as a gemstone. The variety used in jewelry is green or bluish-green and sometimes bears some resemblance to jade. Usually fashioned into cabochons or used as beads, Amazon-stone can easily be distinguished from jade by the flashes of glimmering light seen when the beads are rotated. Handle this and all feldspar minerals with care, because if badly knocked or dropped they can cleave into two parts, leaving clean surfaces.

Fine crystals of Amazon-stone, which despite its name does not come from the Amazon area, are found in Colorado. But much of the material used in jewelry comes from Ontario, Canada, from southern Africa, Russia and Madagascar.

Two other feldspars have joined the gem materials, both used as ornamental stones. They are sunstone and labradorite. The first is a clear oligoclase feldspar, which owes its attractive red and orange color to the spangles of iron oxide it contains. The best of this stone comes from Norway, but Russia and Canada are other sources. Labradorite does indeed come from Labrador, though also from other parts of Canada. Fine material is also found in Finland to which the name spectrolite has been given. Labradorite is gray but when held at certain angles, broad flashes of brilliant reds, orange, blues, greens, purples and yellows are reflected from inside the stone.

Labradorite is rarely used in jewelry, though I have seen a carved piece mounted as a tie pin, which looked very much like a black opal. This stone is more commonly used as an ornamental stone for small objets d'art and inlays. Colorless labradorite with a yellow tinge has been found and fashioned into faceted stones, but it has no commercial significance. It is found in the United States, Mexico and Australia.

8. Zircon and Zoisite

NATURAL ZIRCONS provide a range of stones with a charm of their own. In color they are leaf-green, yellow, brown, olive-green and, more rarely, red. A lovely orange zircon is occasionally found too. But the zircons most commonly mounted in jewelry are sky-blue, golden brown and colorless stones, though their colors are not natural. The brown crystals found in Indo-China change color with careful heat treatment. If they are heated in air so that they become oxidized, these brown crystals become colorless or golden yellow. If heated in a reducing atmosphere, devoid of oxygen, a sky-blue stone generally results. As recently as 1950 the rough crystals were cooked by the natives in crude ovens, but more up-to-date methods are probably used now.

These heat-treated zircons are cut and polished in Bangkok, Thailand, where diamond-charged laps are used, which produce beautifully smooth and brilliant facets on the zircons. Most stones are cut in the brilliant-cut style. More rarely they are shaped in the trap-cut style, though this does not show the zircon's fire at its best—nearly as brilliant as in diamond. Rose-cut colorless zircons, possibly heat-treated Ceylon stones, used in some jewelry of earlier periods, have been mistaken for diamonds.

Zircons are often called jargoons, a term sometimes misused for any white stone impersonating a diamond. With an improved understanding of gemstones, the name jargoon, which used to be correctly applied to any pale-colored zircon, is falling into disuse, as is the name starlite for heat-treated blue zircons.

Heat-treated zircons are rather brittle and the edges of their facets easily chip, if the stones are allowed to rub together. Newly cut zircons exported from Bangkok are therefore wrapped in twists of tissue paper to prevent them touching and abrading each other. Never put zircon jewelry loose with other jewels in a case.

There is another problem with heat-treated zircons. The sky-blue stones and to a lesser extent the colorless ones, tend to revert to their original brownish hue. The blue stones take on a dirty brownish-blue tint, and the colorless stones a brownish tinge. This reversion of color is not thoroughly understood, but is probably caused by some sort of light radiation. Certainly ultra-violet light causes rapid reversion, and sunlight contains much ultra-violet as well as visible light. But not all treated stones revert. The Bangkok merchants usually keep the stones in strong sunlight for a time and pick out those which show signs of turning color. When reversion has taken place it is sometimes possible to bring back the blue color or remove the brownish tinge from colorless stones by careful reheating.

Natural colored zircons are less commonly seen except perhaps for some Ceylonese jewelry, often bought by tourists. An attractive array of handsome green, brown and yellow zircons is set in this, often with rich colored garnets, amethysts and other stones of Ceylon origin.

Apart from the lovely orange zircon, the most attractive stones of this species are the leaf-green ones, characterized by the straight or zoned internal striations, which can be seen with a hand lens.

Many of these leaf-green zircons are particularly interesting scientifically, since, unlike most zircons, they are practically single-refracting and do not show the doubling of the rear facets so obvious in normal zircons. The reason for this is that zircons, particularly those from Ceylon, are radio-active, because of the uranium and thorium they contain. The radio-activity has broken down the crystal structure in these green zircons from a fully crystalized zirconium silicate to a mixture of practically non-crystalline silica and zirconia.

Apart from the heat-treated stones from Indo-China and the variously colored rolled pebbles found in the gem gravels of Ceylon, zircon is found in New South Wales and elsewhere in Australia and in the Mogok Stone Tract of northern Burma. Though zircon, which is usually found in granitic rocks, occurs world-wide, material of gem quality is rarely found other than in those places I've mentioned.

Zircons, particularly when seen in parcels, tend to have a misty or smoky look, though this effect may be apparent in single stones. They have a high luster and most show a large double re-fraction, which may contribute to their misty look. It is also responsible for the doubling of the rear facet edges, seen when they are viewed through the front of the stone with a lens.

The imitation of zircon by other stones is of little importance, except for the blue heat-treated stones, which are well simulated by a suitably colored synthetic spinel and similarly colored glass. Both these stones can be distinguished from zircon by the absence of any doubling of the rear facet edges. Synthetic spinel is also distinguished by the orange residual color it shows when examined through a Chelsea filter.

Zoisite

A new gemstone was brought to light in 1967. This is tanzanite, a transparent form of the mineral zoisite, which was previously known only in its opaque pink rock-like form called thulite, which has been used for inlays in small objets d'art, and also as the bright green rock containing large rubies which is found near Mount Kilimanjaro in Tanzania. This African state also produces the new transparent zoisites, which are violet-blue and sometimes brownish. The magnificent sapphire-blue stones now mounted in jewelry are usually the result of heat treatment, which drives off the colored rays that debase the blue.

Quite large stones have been cut, including a stone of 122.7 carats, now in the collection of the Smithsonian Museum in Washington. Tanzanite rivals the color of sapphire, but is unfortunately too soft a stone to wear well as a ring stone. It is quite acceptable, however, for mounting in earrings, brooches, pendants and other pieces unlikely to be abraded. Tanzanites, still found only near Arusha in Tanzania, can be distinguished from sapphires by the way they change to violet or even brown, when viewed from different angles.

9. Peridot and Spinel

THE BEAUTIFUL OIL-GREEN PERIDOT was an important jewel stone at the beginning of the 19th century. Its popularity then waned for some 50 years and it did not regain favor until the time of Queen Victoria's Jubilee, when many of the older fashions in jewelry were revived. Though not seen as much today as earlier in this century, peridot is still found mounted in jewelry, and large and exceptionally fine peridots command a fair price and have a ready market.

To the mineralogist, this mineral is known as olivine, a name earlier misused for green garnet, properly called demantoid. At one time chrysolite was a popular name for this stone, but it has been used for several other stones and as a prefix to other species with varieties of a yellow-green color. With such confusion the name chrysolite was rightly dropped. Peridot is now the name universally used.

Though the best and most typical color of peridot is oil-green, a yellowish-green or brownish-green hue is more often seen in poorer quality stones, which are less attractive. A true brown peridot is known, though it is quite rare. More will be said of brown peridot later. Peridot is soft compared with other gemstones and therefore less durable. It is thus not suitable as a ring stone, but is a useful addition to the range of jewel stones used for personal jewelry such as necklaces, pendants, brooches and earrings where there is less wear.

Peridot is usually fashioned in the mixed-cut style with a round, oval or drop-shaped outline. Important stones, and some smaller ones are now cut in the trap-cut style. As the stone is so soft, the lapidary often fashions the large table facet with a domed surface. Peridots can also be damaged by a knock, as they cleave easily and stones have been known to part along this line of weakness. Peridot is attacked by acid, particularly sulphuric acid, which will destroy its surface polish fairly rapidly.

The best gem peridots are said to come from Zeberged, an island in the Red Sea better known as the Isle of St. John. This source has been known from very early times, when the stone was probably called topaz, but the site of the deposits was lost for centuries. It was not rediscovered until the beginning of the 20th century. Until 1914, the mines were worked by a French syndicate, but little systematic mining seems to have been done since and most of the important stones in existence are thought to have been recut from older jewels.

Northern Burma produces some fine peridots and stones of a brownish-green shade are found in the gem gravels of Ceylon. Queensland in Australia, Minas Gerais in Brazil, and Norway supply a few peridots as rolled pebbles or crystals. Rounded pebbles of peridots are found in New Mexico and Arizona, often in anthills, having been collected by the industrious ants, like the garnets already mentioned.

Apart from its typical color, peridot shows a large double refraction. This is evidently from the pronounced doubling of the rear facet edges seen with a lens. Before mentioning peridot simulants, it may be interesting to add that up to 1952 many brown and yellowish-brown stones with scientific characteristics close to those of peridots were thought to be iron-rich peridots. But these so-called brown peridots were subsequently found to be an entirely new mineral, to which the name sinhalite was given. Sinhalites are less rare than true brown peridots.

Peridot Simulants

Very fine imitations of peridot are made in glass (paste). A synthetic corundum of near peridot color is also produced. Other simulants are a soudé type of stone made from synthetic spinel and a similar colored garnet-topped doublet. The pastes and composite stones are easy to detect, as they do not show doubling of the rear facet edges. Corundum shows this effect only weakly and cannot be confused with the well separated double edges shown by true peridot.

Spinel

Spinels include a wide range of colors from red to violet. Other common hues of this gemstone used in jewelry are blue and purple. Yellow and brown stones are seldom seen and green stones, called ceylonites, are usually far too dark to make attractive gems, as they look nearly black. There are true black spinels too, which have occasionally been cut to form stones for mourning jewelry.

The red and blue stones, some of the latter purplish in artificial light, are the most important in jewelry. Spinels do not, however, quite reach the splendor of ruby and sapphire. In olden days the red stones were called Balas rubies or spinel rubies, names which by common consent and modern legislation have now been abandoned.

Spinel forms octahedral crystals, shaped like two of the Egyptian pyramids base to base. This is a form also taken by diamond. In Northern Burma, small bright red octahedral crystals with brilliant faces are found. They have been mounted in jewelry with one point of the crystal uppermost, without further embellishment. Large spinel crystals are not so common but some large stones are known, notably the Black Prince's Ruby, which has an exciting history. This stone now graces the Imperial State Crown of the British Regalia though it is not a ruby but a red spinel. The stone is mounted in its natural crystal form, and, apart from having been drilled so that it could be tied to clothing, a method of fixing common to early Indian jewels, has only been polished on the faces. It is not faceted. The drilled hole is now filled with a small ruby.

Another historical spinel is the Timur Ruby, which was presented to Queen Victoria in 1851. With a history going back over 600 years, this stone is engraved with Persian script and is said to weigh 361 carats. It was at one time thought to be the largest red spinel known. This is now disputed, for the red spinel in the crown of Catherine II, now in the Diamond Treasury in Moscow, is said to weigh over 400 carats.

Rather like almandine and pyrope garnets, spinels, which consist of a double oxide of magnesium and aluminum, may have their magnesium replaced by zinc to produce a variety which goes by the name gahno-spinel. This is of more interest to the scientist than the buyer of jewel stones. When the change from magnesium to zinc is complete, these zinc spinels are called gahnite, but the green crystals are only cut to satisfy the collector's whim.

Spinel is found worldwide, but the main localities for gem crystals are Burma and Ceylon. It is also grown synthetically in a number of colors, though these synthetic stones do not generally display the same hues as natural spinel. Their colors are usually imitations of other species of stones, particularly aquamarines, blue zircons and sapphires, but also green tourmaline. Bright colorless stones are also produced, which are used to simulate diamond in cheaper jewelry.

Other colors made are a fine pink, a red and a yellow to greenish-yellow. Blue synthetic spinels which imitate aquamarine, zircon and sapphire are easily identified by the red or orange residual color seen when they are viewed through a Chelsea color filter. Stones imitating green tourmaline do not show the doubling of the rear facets like the real stone. Colorless spinel is not found in nature and yellow and yellow-green synthetic spinels show a fluorescent effect. This shimmering apple-green fluorescence can be seen in daylight, but is most brilliant under an ultra-violet lamp.

The famous Russian jeweler Carl Fabergé made flowers in precious metals set with gemstones like this lily of the valley. The glass and water are rock crystal.

10. Amethyst and Other Quartzes

PROBABLY ONE of the earliest minerals to be used for ornamentation was quartz. Many ancient Greek and Roman intaglios and cameos were carved in forms of this mineral. There are many forms of quartz, among them the beautiful violet or purple amethyst, the yellow citrine and one of a brown or smoky brown color, known as cairngorm or smoky quartz. I must also mention the lovely rose quartz, and at least two types of green quartz.

Rock Crystal

The purest form of quartz is the water-white variety called rock crystal. Its beautiful lustrous hexagonal prisms, forming groups of crystals found in rock cavities, were in early times thought to be water, frozen too hard ever to melt. Rock crystal is a fairly common mineral and scarcely pays for the cost of faceting, but many of the rondels (disk-shaped stones) strung between the beads in some stone necklaces are rock crystal. Its outstanding artistic use is making carved figurines and other ornaments.

Many gem minerals are also important in science and industry. This is certainly true of rock crystal. Its internal atomic pattern has a peculiar screw-like formation which produces special optical and physical effects. Rock crystal exhibits a piezo-electric effect. That is, when pressure is applied in certain definite directions an electric charge is induced at each end of the axis of pressure. Conversely, if an electric current is applied across a suitably cut plate of rock crystal, it will vibrate at a certain frequency.

This effect is used to control radio frequencies and to maintain the accuracy of so-called quartz clocks and watches, accurate to about a minute a year. Quartz is hard enough to be used in many instruments where a hard-bearing surface is needed. Its transparency to ultra-violet light also qualifies it for use in certain scientific instruments.

As it grows, a crystal of colorless quartz can surround minerals formed earlier, to produce attractive specimens, some of which have been used as gemstones. For instance, rock crystal may enclose needle-like crystals of black tourmaline or green actinolite. But the best known is rock crystal that encloses fine hair-like crystals of reddish-brown rutile. This rutilated quartz, sometimes called Venus'-hair stone or Thetis'-hair stone (after the goddesses of classic myth), makes a distinctive gemstone. When long needles of leek-green actinolite are thickly disseminated throughout rock crystal, a stone called plasma results. A great variety of minerals can be included in quartz, of which I can mention but a few. Blue chrysocolla may impregnate rock crystal and is cut and polished as cabochons. So can dumortierite and cinnabar, which produce dark blue and pink stones respectively.

The most important sources of rock crystal are Brazil, Japan, Burma, Switzerland and the United States, though the crystals are found worldwide. Usually free of obvious imperfections, rock crystal may sometimes contain "feathers." These feathers would be undesirable in some articles, such as crystal balls, but in carved pieces can be a useful sign that the piece is genuine and not glass. Feathers in the two pieces in rock crystal used for the soudé emerald, help give this composite gemstone a natural appearance. Some rock crystal contains very thin, flat cavities, which may produce interference colors, like those seen on a soap bubble. This flawed rock crystal is known as iris quartz. Sometimes these cracks are produced artificially by heating the rock crystal and then rapidly cooling it in cold water, which sometimes contains a dye that enters the cracks. This produces the gems we call firestones.

Amethyst

Amethyst, the violet-colored quartz, varies from stones nearly devoid of color and of little value, to those of a rich velvety purple. Amethyst's popularity has fluctuated considerably at different times, but the deep purple stones are rare enough to hold their value. Amethyst is usually fashioned in the mixed-cut style with a round, oval or sometimes heart-shaped outline. But the trap-cut style is now more commonly used for important stones and some are cut as cabochons or beads. Much amethyst-set jewelry of Victorian and earlier times will be seen to have the table facets of the stones cut with a domed surface, not flat as in modern stones. Flawed and unevenly colored material is used for carvings.

A popular stone for ecclesiastical jewelry, particularly for bishops' rings, amethyst is found in many parts of the world. Most of the better quality amethyst comes from near Rivera and Artigas in Uruguay and the neighboring area in southern Brazil. Amethysts found near Sverdlovsk in the Ural Mountains of Russia are rich purple but tend to take on a crimson hue when viewed in artificial light. Amethyst crystals are also found in many parts of the United States and at Thunder Bay on the north

shore of Lake Superior in Canada, as well as in Madagascar, Rhodesia and the Republic of South Africa, including a source of beautiful colored material inland from the Skeleton Coast of northern South-West Africa. There are deposits in Japan and China and others have recently been found in Western Australia.

Sark stones are poor quality amethysts at one time found in the island of Sark in the Channel Islands group. This source is now exhausted and the Sark stones sold to tourists are cut from South American crystals. Some poor quality amethyst may also be found in Cornwall and Ireland.

Like rock crystal, amethyst may enclose other minerals. Interesting stones are cut from amethyst containing groups of needle-like crystals of cacoxenite arranged in sheaves. A lens will often reveal a typical thumbprint pattern in amethyst. This is sometimes referred to as a ripple fracture or tiger marking and is conclusive evidence of the genuineness of amethyst. Alternate areas of colored and colorless stone can be seen in amethyst. In a cut stone, patches of color may be angular or in bands. By careful cutting the color patches may be arranged so that the finished stone looks uniformly colored. The reason for the amethyst's beautiful hue is not fully understood, though many theories have been put forward to account for it.

Some amethyst shows a striking change of color after it has been subjected to moderate heat. It usually turns yellow or orange-yellow, but occasionally becomes green, though the green seems less stable than the yellow. Much amethyst is burnt, and burnt amethysts have been cut and sold as topaz, quartz topaz or topaz quartz, names which are now forbidden by law. These stones are better known as golden quartz. Some attempt was made to market greened amethysts under the name prasiolite, but as they tend to fade, their commercialization seems to have failed.

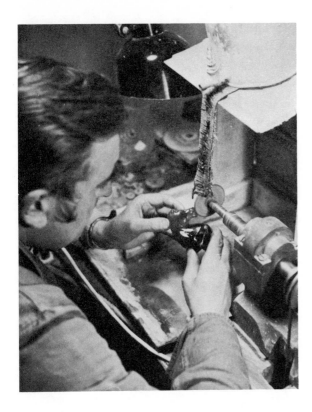

Gem minerals are cut with a rotating wheel and wet abrasive powder. A knight of a chess set is being carved in smoky quartz in the gem cutting center of Idar-Oberstein in West Germany.

If colored quartz is overheated, it discolors and finally crazes, giving a schiller effect. Such stones are produced and cut as cabochons to imitate moonstones. Bearing in mind that amethyst changes color when heated, never lay jewelry set with amethysts on a warm or hot stove, or their color may start to change.

The most common imitation of amethyst is glass, but this will feel warm to the touch. Natural and synthetic stones will feel cold. Other simulations of amethyst are a suitably colored synthetic sapphire and a similarly colored soudé-type of stone. A garnet-topped doublet with a base of amethyst-colored glass is known. A stone with an amethyst-colored glass base and a quartz top is another freak composite stone you may see. The only natural stones which can be mistaken for amethysts are violet and purple sapphires and some kunzites, though certain garnets and spinels can also approach the color of amethyst.

Citrine

The yellow quartz called citrine varies from light yellow to reddish-yellow. It is rarer in nature than other colors of quartz. Practically all the yellow quartz on the market is the result of heat-treating amethyst or sometimes brown quartz. The best citrine comes from Brazil, but small quantities are found in Russia, Madagascar and Spain, where a fine wine-colored orange-yellow material was once found.

Imitations of yellow quartz are glass, a synthetic yellow sapphire and a yellow soudé stone made to imitate citrine. Any natural yellow stone may resemble citrine, but particularly stones with a luster near that of quartz, such as yellow feldspar, yellow beryl, yellow tourmaline and topaz.

Other Colors

Far more common than yellow quartz is brown quartz, which can vary from light brown to a brown so dark as to appear black. This nearly black quartz is called morion. Some brownish quartz has a smoky tinge and is called smoky quartz. Much brown quartz used to be found in the Cairngorm mountains in the Scottish Highlands, which earned the name cairngorm. This Scottish source of this color quartz is now practically exhausted and most brown quartz comes from Brazil and Switzerland, the United States of America, Japan and Australia.

White quartz, commonly known as milky quartz, owes its milky-white color to myriads of tiny cavities in the stone. It is this type of quartz which forms veins in rock formations. Vein quartz from some sources may contain flecks of gold, and is sometimes cut into plates or cabochons and mounted in jewelry. This is the only kind of milky quartz used in jewelry.

The attractive rose quartz is used for carving into small figurines or other objets d'art. Occasionally carved or cabochon-cut pieces are mounted in jewelry, and exceptionally clear pieces have been faceted. Rose quartz varies from almost white to deep rose-pink and the deeper its hue, the more highly prized the stone. This material is rarely found in crystals, but usually as veins. It is nearly always cloudy, owing to the many fissures it contains, which give it a milky appearance and often add to its attractiveness. The color, said to be due to a trace of titanium, often tends to fade. Some rose quartz contains oriented needle-like inclusions of rutile and shows a star effect. This is used in the composite stone made to imitate the star sapphire. Brazil, the United States and Rössing in South-West Africa are the best known localities for rose quartz.

Yellow, brownish- or grayish-green quartz, containing a multitude of fine parallel asbestos fibers, when cut as cabochon cat's-eyes, can resemble the true chrysoberyl cat's-eyes, though the ray is usually less sharp. Quartz cat's-eyes are found in the gem gravels of Ceylon and in the Fichtelgebirge in Bavaria, as well as in India. Another type of quartz cat's-eye is known as crocidolite or more widely as tiger's-eye. The best material is golden yellow with a silky banded luster. This is actually a form of asbestos called crocidolite, which has been replaced particle by particle with quartz, while the silky structure of the original material remains. The mineralogist calls this a pseudomorph of quartz after crocidolite. The golden yellow of tiger's-eye is due to the oxidation of the iron in the original crocidolite which is bluish green.

A similar quartz replacement where the original color has not been altered by oxidation gives the so-called hawk's-eye. The main sources of tiger's-eye used for jewelry are in Cape Province, near Griqualand and just north of the Orange River, in South Africa. Crocidolite can be stained, usually blue or green. A red color is obtained by heating the golden tiger's-eye.

Quartzite

Another type of quartz we must consider is quartzite, a rock of more or less pure quartz, which in its various forms is often used for beads and cabochons and carvings. Quartzite is scientifically known as a metamorphic rock, for it results from the alteration of sandstone by the heat and pressure of an intruding mass of extremely hot, viscous primary rock, which welled up from the hot inner core of the earth. Such a geological disturbance alters the structure of the sandstone to form interlocking crystals of quartz.

Pure quartzite is white, but the rock is usually completely or patchily colored with impurities, particularly flaky minerals such as mica and hematite, which have crystallized between the irregular crystals of the main mass. These inclusions often give it a spangled appearance, and it is then known as aventurine quartz.

Green aventurine quartz, which owes its color to flakes of green mica included in the rock, is the form most commonly met in jewelry. The amount of mica present can vary enormously. Some material is white with a few green patches, but there can be sufficient mica to give the rock a uniform bright green color. Some may be so heavily impregnated and banded with mica that it resembles the green copper mineral called malachite. The most important source of green aventurine quartz is India.

In another type of aventurine quartz, the flakes are of the iron mineral called hematite, which give the stone a pale brownish-red hue. This material, sometimes called eosite, is mostly used for carvings, bowls and vases. There is a fine large vase cut from brownish aventurine quartz in the main hall of the Museum of the Institute of Geological Sciences at South Kensington, London. The material from which it was carved came from the Korgon Mountains in Siberia. Other varieties of quartzite include a gray type from Chile, and an attractive brown rock from Cape de Gata in Southern Spain, but these do not seem to have been much used artistically.

Synthetic Quartz

Quartz crystals have been grown artificially and this synthetic rock crystal is used for scientific and industrial purposes. Some blue, green, and golden yellow quartz, and even amethyst-colored quartz, has also been produced synthetically and cut, polished and mounted in jewelry, though it is not common. Some really splendid gold quartz recently encountered may have been produced by irradiation with cobalt 60.

An area in Lightning Ridge, Australia, where opal miners have worked, is like a moon landscape. Opal is found here and at White Cliffs in New South Wales, Coober Pedy and Andamooka in South Australia, and Quilpie in Queensland. There are areas where diamonds are being mined in Lesotho (formerly Basutoland), southern Africa, 10,000 feet (3,000 m.) high in the mountains, that look just like this opal field.

All the small stones at the top of this picture are diamonds, brilliant cut to give the maximum effect. All the larger stones below are opals. Those with a dark ground are known as black opals and those with a white ground as white opals.

In the top two rows are amethysts, a form of
purple quartz which can also be much lighter
in color than the specimens shown here. The
next row is of smoky quartz and the bottom two
rows of a form of yellow or golden quartz called
citrine.

11. Opal

THE KALEIDOSCOPIC CHANGES of color so characteristic of opal are not seen in any other gemstones—they are displayed only by the prized precious opal. There are many so-called common opals, which, though they do not show the play of color of the precious kind, should not be entirely discounted, for some of the more attractive of them have been mounted in jewelry.

Opal is a romantic stone that has had many vicissitudes in its long history. In ancient times it was believed to have the virtues of all the stones whose colors appeared in it. Superstition was rife then, and the many-colored opal must have had many beneficial influences ascribed to it. For this reason alone it must have been highly prized. Opals were considered to be especially potent in preventing or curing eye diseases and were said to increase the wearer's keenness of vision, while dimming that of the onlooker. One benefit ascribed to opal, of the greatest value to the wearer, though surely not to society, was that it could make a thief invisible, so he could go about his work unhindered.

The superstition that opal brings misfortune, so prevalent during the 19th century, is now fast disappearing. This fear of opal was comparatively recent, for in the Middle Ages and earlier this stone was held in high favor. Even in the 17th century, opal was held in greater esteem than now. Authorities differ as to how and when the superstition arose. It may have originated from an old German superstition, or perhaps from Sir Walter Scott's novel *Anne of Geierstein*, in which opal played such a malignant part.

Scott may even have got his idea of an opal of evil influence from some already existent belief.

Opal is an amorphous form of hydrated silica and contains about 8 per cent of water. It is a hardened gel deposited from a silica-rich solution as a secondary formation, filling seams and fissures in any of the three main types of rock. In geological terms it is a young mineral formed comparatively recently. Opal may be opaque or transparent.

The glorious flashes of color that the precious opal displays are due to a special optical effect, known as interference of light at thin films. This occurs when a ray of light meets a very thin film of a substance with a different optical density from that of the main mass. The colors of a soap bubble or a film of oil on water are created in the same way. Precious opal contains a great number of these thin films, shown by recent research to be very thin layers of sub-microscopic spheres. It displays many flashes of color which vary as the stone is turned.

You can prove that this play of color is optical in nature by looking through the stone towards a light. The opal then appears a dingy yellow. A second optical effect can be seen in opal, whether precious or common—a cloudy look, like that seen in slightly milky glass. The result of light reflection from sub-microscopic particles, it is known as opalescence.

The historical source of opal is the mines in the Libánka and Simonka Mountains, north of Kosice in the eastern part of Czechoslovakia. These Slovak mines were formerly under Hungarian rule, so the stones were, and still are, called Hungarian opals. The Romans obtained their opals from these eastern European mines and, though there was a notion that opal was known to the classical Greeks, it is unlikely that it was known before 150 B.C. The Romans probably did not know of it until they conquered Corinth. This brought them into direct contact with Byzantium (now Istanbul), then the gateway to the Black Sea and Dacia, now northern Romania, beyond which lay the opal mines.

These deposits were worked successfully by the local peasants from about the 14th century, but in 1788 the government nationalized the mines and started underground workings. This venture was not successful and was soon abandoned. Several decades later the mines were farmed out to individual miners, who worked them until the rich Australian fields were discovered. Czechoslovakian opal has a milk-white background upon which small points of many different colors produce a harlequin effect. It is found in nests in a grayish-brown andesite rock of volcanic origin.

Mexico is the next country to consider as a producer of opal. The stone is believed to have been known to the Aztecs as early as the 13th century. The opal is found in cavities in silica-rich volcanic lavas and is recovered by conventional mining methods, using rock drilling and blasting. This often shatters the opal. Cracking open the matrix with hammers to see if it contains opal does further damage. The opal is principally obtained from the state of Queretaro, but other Mexican states also produce it. The town of Queretaro is the center of the opal trade and the stones are cut and polished there. Though the cutters use only crude home-constructed cutting benches, they turn out quite good polished specimens.

The most important type of opal found in Mexico is the clear orange or yellow, which sometimes shows a play of color too and is called cherry opal in the United States and fire opal in England. Americans use the term fire opal for precious opal. The term cherry opal is confusing as there is also a common opal of cherry-red color which has been cut in cabochon form. Cherry opal is found in a trachyte porphyry in Hidalgo state.

Another opal is the so-called water opal, a clear stone showing a play of color, and which without this play of color would be the fairly common mineral hyalite. A really splendid example of water opal, with its magnificent iridescent colors, is a joy to look upon. Much precious opal is found in Mexico, but it does not reach the quality of the opal found in Australia. A lot of Mexican opal is non-iridescent common opal, which can have a bright yellow, reddish or violet body color. It is often cut as cabochons, and makes attractive stones.

Gracios o Dios and other places in Honduras may well have been the source of the opal used by the Quiche Indians of Colombia. But Honduras opal and the relatively small amount found in Guatemala have scant commercial importance.

Australia undoubtedly yields the finest opal. The first reported occurrence of this stone in Australia was in 1849, when it was found in South Australia, but the discovery of boulder opal at Listowel Downs in 1872 was really the beginning of the Australian opal fields. The opal found there occurs in thin veins in boulders of a hard brown jasper rock. In 1877, opal was found in a soft vesicular basalt by a tributary of the Abercrombie River east of Sydney, New South Wales.

The first really important discovery of opal in Australia also occurred in the state of New South Wales in 1899, when four prospectors following a wounded kangaroo came across loose opal on the ground. This float opal indicated that more opal was beneath the surface. Thus were discovered the famed White Cliffs opal

Opal is found underground 20 to 30 feet (6 to 9 meters) down and hauled to the surface by winch. Two men usually work a claim, one below with pick and kerosene lamp to spot the opal seam. Their only other tool is a shovel. This scene is at White Cliffs, Australia.

fields, some 130 miles (208 km) northeast of Broken Hill in the western part of the state.

The White Cliffs opal is cream in color and is found in seams in sandstone. About 27 to 39 feet (8 to 12 meters) beneath the surface is a band of fine-grained siliceous sandstone, called bandstone. This contains no opal, but guides the miners, since it acts as a horizon to the opal-bearing rocks. Above and below it are clayey sandstones in which the opal is found, more abundantly in the lower than the upper rock.

The opal is found in thin veins in the bedding planes of the sandstone. Not all the veins contain the colorful precious opal, for gem-quality opal occurs as irregular patches in the so-called potch, which forms the bulk of the vein opal. Potch is opal that does not show the play of color or, as

the miners say, is not alive. Attractive opalized fossils, which make fine museum specimens, are also found at White Cliffs.

At Tintenbar in New South Wales, five miles from Ballina, an opal is found with a transparent matrix upon which the colors flash out. It resembles the Mexican water opal, but unfortunately tends to craze. There are a number of other less important deposits of opal in New South Wales.

The famed black opal of Australia, whose unique beauty stems from its colors in all their scintillating beauty, occurring in a somber background or matrix, comes from the Lightning Ridge deposit. This ridge is just a bulge from the plains near the town of Walgett in the northwest of New South Wales. The opal is found at varying depths, from a foot below the surface and to as much as 80 feet (24 meters). Unlike the White Cliffs seam opal, the black opal of Lightning Ridge is found as nodules comparable in size and shape to olives. The local miners call these "nobbies."

The Hayricks opal mine of Queensland is found amid a striking group of sandstone mesas. The mine lies near Quilpie, 700 miles (1120 km) from Brisbane and the opal is found in cracks in ironstone boulders. Other less important deposits of opal exist in the desert area of south-central Queensland.

In 1914, opals were found at Coober Pedy in the Stuart Range in South Australia. Occurring with gypsum in sandstone, the Stuart Range opal is of good quality, but tends to crack when brought up into the hot atmosphere. At Andamooka, some 270 miles (432 km) southeast of Coober Pedy, an opal deposit was found in 1930. The opal lies not far from the surface and some fine black opal has been mined. Much of the Andamooka opal shows green flashes of color, and as this color is most prized by the Japanese, most of this opal is exported to Japan. The lovely Andamooka opal, which weighed some 6 oz. (168 grams) when rough and 203 carats when cut, came from this locality. This magnificent opal was presented to Her Majesty Queen Elizabeth II, after being set as the center drop in a necklace.

Fifteen years later, opal of a quite different kind was found at Andamooka, 300 miles (480 km) north of Coober Pedy. This opal is semi-transparent with a strong blue body color and a stronger green play of color. Another type of opal sometimes encountered is opal matrix, where iridescent patches of precious opal are cut together with the sandstone or dark brown ironstone matrix. The opal and ironstone have often impregnated the gidgee-tree, a type of acacia. These are called gidgee opals.

Some opal from Andamooka, of such poor quality that it was formerly discarded, has in recent years been treated by a form of carbon staining. This gives the tone a black background, but it makes a poor imitation of black opal. These treated opals are unique in showing a play of color in a mosaic of small patches of color, a feature which clearly identifies them.

Except for the Hayrick opal mine, where the opal is won by tunneling into the hillside, Australian opal is mined by simply sinking a shaft down to the band of hard rock. Penetration of this hard rock, known as "shincracker," because pieces of it fly off and hit his shins when the miner swings his pick, brings the miner to the opal dirt, his name for the opal-bearing stratum.

North American sources of opal are many, but most produce only forms of common opal without any play of color. Some precious opal is found at Virgin Valley and Rainbow Ridge in Nevada, from which localities some fine opal has been won, though this stone tends to crack. The opal found near Caballo in New Mexico is lemon-yellow and golden-orange and varies from translucent to opaque. But much American opal is fossil wood, in which the original wood has been replaced by opal, leaving the original structure readily discernible. Some white common opal contains tree-like black markings. All these can make attractive ornamental stones. A green common opal, called chloropal, gets its color from inclusions of a nickel mineral. Some of it can be cut as cabochons and then resembles chrysoprase.

Except for fire opal, the cabochon cut is universally used for fashioning opal. But fire opal is often faceted in the mixed-cut or trap-cut styles and its table facet is often domed. Opal is sometimes carved into leaf forms for mounting into jewelry, but carved opals are rare because of their strong tendency to crack.

A father and son work an underground claim at Lightning Ridge, the only main source of black opal. The candles enable them to spot the glint of opal in the sandstone walls and roof, which they gouge out with picks.

Simulants

Thin seams of precious opal are often cut complete with the sandstone or ironstone matrix at the back to give the stone solidity. They may seem to resemble doublets, unless the junction of the opal and matrix is closely examined. True opal doublets are thin slices of opal cemented on to a backing of potch opal or glass. In black opal doublets, a black glass called opalite is usually used, but sometimes the backing is of black onyx. Opal doublets may be obvious when unset, but it is hard to be sure when they are set without first removing them from their setting.

A new type of composite opal is made by taking an ordinary opal doublet, usually with a backing of potch opal, and fitting a cabochon of rock crystal to the front of it like a cover-glass on a microscope. These triplex opals, as they are known, may appear brighter than opals without such a cover, and the opal is protected from damage. Water opals are often set in a closed setting with a piece of purple silk beneath the stone. This enhances the stone's appearance and its play of color.

There are no convincing imitation opals. Many attempts have been made to make a paste opal, but none has been satisfactory. One consists of a hollow cabochon of glass in which twisted pieces of colored foil have been placed. A piece of glass or rock crystal backed by a piece of mother-of-pearl cut from the colorful abalone shell makes a better imitation. Labradorite feldspar with its brilliant flashes of color can resemble opal, particularly when the piece is carved, so that the broad areas of color are broken up to some extent. Synthetic opal has been made and is now on the commercial market.

12. Some Lesser-Known Gemstones

SOME 150 MINERALS or varieties of mineral have been cut and polished, many of them solely at the whim of collectors. Relatively few of them have joined those gems used for adornment. In this chapter I shall discuss some of the more important of these rarer kinds of stone.

Kunzite

This stone, the lilac-pink form of the mineral spodumene, has some prestige in jewelry, particularly in North America. Its color varies from a bluish-pink to a rich pure pink and may resemble pink beryl and pink topaz. Indeed, it may take more than mere inspection to differentiate between them. The major sources of kunzite are the Pala district of California, Brazil and the island of Madagascar. Other colors of spodumene occur, notably yellow, but as yellow stones are quite common in other better known species, yellow spodumene has nothing fresh to offer. Green-colored stones are more important. These vary from a rare grass-green—stones that are correctly called hiddenite, and closely resemble emerald—to paler, more yellowish green, of which large stones occur in Brazil. These are usually called hiddenite too, though true hiddenite is only found in small stones in North Carolina.

Sphene

This stone is characterized by having a greater fire than diamond, though the effect is masked by the stone's green, yellow or brown color. Cut stones always appear a little hazy owing to their very strong double refraction, much greater than that of zircon, so the back facets appear more doubled and more easily seen than in zircon. Unfortunately sphene is a soft stone and therefore not durable enough to wear well. If it were not for this, it would make a splendid addition to the range of gemstones. Sphene comes from Burma, Mexico (Lower California), Switzerland and the Austrian Tyrol.

Scapolite

White, pink and mauve stones showing chatoyancy, the cat's-eye effect, are probably the best known forms of this mineral. But these stones, which come mostly from Burma, are more for those who seek the unusual than for the general buyer of jewelry. Yellow varieties of scapolite come from Brazil and Mozambique, but the stones are of scant importance in jewelry.

Andalusite

The most common colors of this mineral are greenish-brown and brownish-green. These stones come from Brazil and show an interesting two-color effect. There is also a much rarer form, again from Brazil, of a bright green, rarely seen as cut stones and of no importance in jewelry. Some andalusite crystals are opaque and unusual in revealing carbonaceous inclusions in the shape of a cross when the crystal is cut across. When cut to show this effect, these stones are often called cross stones, though correctly termed chiastolite. They are often sold as amulets.

Apatite

Apatite is found in a great variety of colors, but is far too soft to make a satisfactory gemstone. The main colors are yellow, green, blue and violet—there seem to be no red apatites. Some show a cat's-eye effect when cut into cabochons, and pale blue apatites showing this effect do make attractive stones. Apatite occurs worldwide, but gem material comes mostly from Brazil, Burma, Canada, Mexico and the United States of America. This mineral is composed of calcium phosphate and it may interest you to know that the dentine of teeth is mainly apatite.

Axinite

Though hard enough to produce a satisfactory gemstone, axinite suffers from its drab clove-brown hue. Few stones are cut from the rather flat crystals, except for collectors, and this stone is unlikely to be mounted in jewelry. It occurs in France and the United States, but the largest crystals come from Lower California, Mexico.

Benitoite

This stone was first found in San Benito County, California in 1908, when it was at first thought to be sapphire, which it closely resembles, despite its violet tinge. In this it more nearly resembles the new blue zoisite called tanzanite, except that tanzanite is found in large crystals, while the largest benitoite stone reported is not more than seven carats. California is the only known source.

Danburite

Some magnificent yellow stones have been cut from crystals of danburite, which is hard enough to stand up to wear. It could rival topaz if it were not so scarce. There is also a less attractive colorless variety, but it is merely another colorless stone with no special merit. The best danburite comes from Burma, but some colorless crystals are found in Japan and Mexico.

Diopside

Diopside is characterized by its green hue, though there are some brown stones. The green stones are sometimes cut and have been mounted in jewelry, when they are usually trap-cut. Some diopside has fibrous inclusions which produce a cat's-eye effect. These, too, are sometimes met in jewelry. Recently a very dark green to nearly black diopside has come from India. When cut in the cabochon style, it shows a four-rayed star of light. Such star diopsides have been mounted in jewelry and if the stones are not in a mount and are placed with the domed top downwards on a polished surface and a magnet placed near the edge of the stone, the stone will rotate as the inclusions causing the star are magnetic. Other forms of diopside are found in Burma, Russia, East Africa, Canada and mixed with diamond in the Kimberley diamond mines.

Phenakite

Phenakite is often mistaken for rock crystal as there is some similarity in the form of the crystals. Indeed, the name phenakite comes from a Greek word meaning "deceptive." Phenakites are colorless, though pale pink stones have been reported yet never seen. This gives some credence to the suggestion that pink crystals quickly fade on exposure to light. Quite recently a greenish-blue phenakite has turned up, but it is not known where it came from. Some wine-yellow crystals have been reported from Russia. The only stones which are occasionally met in jewelry are colorless phenakites. Although colorless, they are especially lustrous stones. Gem quality crystals are found in Brazil, eastern and southern Africa and in the United States.

Iolite

Sometimes known as cordierite, iolites are always blue and may resemble sapphire, but owing to their strong directional color (dichroism) may appear more akin to the new blue zoisite, tanzanite. Iolites are sometimes seen in jewelry, but are not popular. Gem iolites come from Burma, India and Ceylon. Some of these Ceylon stones contain masses of platelets of an iron mineral, which give them a red hue—one writer nicknamed them blood-shot iolites.

Enstatite

Green and brown enstatites resemble diopsides and are related to them mineralogically. As with diopside, a bright green variety is found with diamond in the Kimberley diamond mines. Enstatite also produces star stones, which are dark brown to black and show a six-rayed star. Apart from South Africa, Burma and Ceylon are the main sources of enstatite, which is unimportant as a gemstone.

Idocrase

This is not an important gemstone, as its green, greenish-brown and brown colors make little appeal, apart perhaps, from the brown stones found in Canada, and the massive green ones. The massive green variety, which can closely resemble jade, is probably the most important as gem material. Massive green idocrase readily forms rock mixtures with massive green grossular garnet, which are now frequently carved into ornaments and figures. It is difficult to identify such a rock mixture accurately and say whether it contains mostly idocrase, when it could be called massive idocrase, or mostly grossular, when it should be classed as massive grossular. Although it can easily be proved that this material is not

jade, it would not be easy to assign a specific name to it. Such material comes from California and Pakistan.

Euclase

This rare mineral shows such a strong cleavage that cutting the stone is hazardous. A beautiful greeny-blue, somewhat resembling aquamarine, euclase has been mounted in jewelry. If of some size, euclases make magnificent stones, but small stones lack the richness of color of the larger ones. Brazil is the main source, though some crystals have been found in Africa.

Epidote

Epidote, a stone allied to zoisite, is of minor importance in jewelry, owing to its rather somber brownish or pistachio-green. It is found worldwide.

Kyanite

Kyanite is sapphire blue in its gem variety, but this fairly common mineral varies from colorless to sapphire blue, or greenish-blue. Crystals of kyanite are harder across their width than along their length. This and the readiness with which the mineral cleaves, makes the cutting of kyanite into gemstones most difficult—it is cut almost entirely for collectors. The best gem material comes from Burma and East Africa. Kyanite is actually more important for making high temperature ceramics than for gemstones.

Fibrolite

A similar material to kyanite, to which it is chemically related, fibrolite or sillimanite, as it is sometimes called, also resembles kyanite in being blue. Good crystals are rarely found, for most are fibrous, a feature which gives this mineral its name. Again like kyanite, it cleaves readily, which makes it difficult to cut as a gemstone. It has no particular value in jewelry, but massive varieties of fibrolite, usually called sillimanite, of greenish or brownish color, have been used in imitation of jade, and also tumble-polished to produce baroque stones.

Kornerupine

Appreciated more by the collector than the jeweler and his customer, kornerupine can be green or brownish-green. Some kornerupines have been found with a star effect and may turn up mounted in jewelry. Star kornerupines, and even cat's-eye kornerupines, which are also known, could make useful jewelry stones. Ceylon, Burma, Madagascar, and eastern Africa are the best known sources.

Brazilianite

First discovered in 1944, brazilianite provides stones of a lemon-yellow hue. When first found, the crystals were thought to be chrysoberyl, until a mineralogist saw them and realized that they were the wrong shape for chrysoberyl. Some effort was made to market the stones as gems, but, short of interested collectors, there was no market for a stone which had no distinct difference from the many other yellow stones. Brazil, where it was first found, and New Hampshire are the only known localities.

Cassiterite

Mainly cut for collectors, the transparent brown form of the usually black mineral cassiterite, the oxide of tin, which is of more importance as an ore of that metal, is not worth much consideration here. This mineral occurs worldwide, but the crystals are only transparent enough to be worth cutting in a few places.

Chrysocolla

As a gem material, chrysocolla has scant importance, except when impregnating rock crystal or chalcedony, when it produces a fine green or blue material suitable for cutting into cabochons. Chrysocolla is a copper mineral that, when mixed with other copper minerals, forms a variegated green, blue and black rock, which is cut into cabochons or polished by the tumbling method. One example of this rock is found at the so-called King Solomon's mines near Eilat, Israel, at the head of the Gulf of Aqaba. Appropriately named Eilat stone, polished stones are sold to tourists and even exported for sale in Western countries.

Smithsonite

Named after James Smithson, founder of the Smithsonian Institution in Washington, smithsonite in its bluish-green variety has been cut as a cabochon and used as a gemstone. This particular variety comes from the Kelly Mine in New Mexico, U.S.A. Beyond its attractive color, the stone has little to recommend it. It can be damaged by acids and is characterized by a rather high density, so that the stone can be identified by its weight in the hand.

Chlorastrolite

The stone called chlorastrolite is characterized by its radial structure. Made up of interlocking groups of radial crystals, this green stone is obvious once a sample has been seen. Chlorastrolites are found as rolled pebbles on the shores of Lake Superior.

Thomsonite

A stone rather similar to chlorastrolite, thomsonite usually has a white background upon which is a pattern of red- or green-bordered eyes. Some stones are just brown and white and less attractive. Like chlorastrolite, thomsonite is found along the shores of Lake Superior.

Zinc-Blende

Also known as sphalerite, zinc-blende, which is an ore of zinc, is black and quite unsuitable as a gemstone. But fairly clear pieces of a brownish yellow can be obtained in two localities, and some faceted stones have been cut from them, mainly to satisfy collectors. The stones have a very good fire, some three times greater than that of diamond, though their color masks the effect. The stones have a resinous luster and cleave very easily, so cutting is very difficult. Mexico and Spain are the two sources of transparent zinc-blende.

Staurolite

Rarely cut as a gemstone, staurolite is nonetheless especially attractive by reason of the peculiar shapes assumed by the crystals. The prismatic crystals tend to grow in pairs, crossing one another at 60 degrees or a right angle. This produces the so-called cross stone. Such twinned crystals, as the crystallographer calls them, are sold as amulets, with or without the faces of the brown crystals polished. Staurolite is found in many places, but France, Switzerland and North America may be singled out.

13. Chalcedony, Agate and Jasper

CHALCEDONY takes many forms, from the popular banded material which is the best-known agate, through many forms and colors to the heavily pigmented massive quartz called jasper, which is not a true chalcedony but conveniently fits into this chapter.

Chalcedony is made up of a vast number of extremely small quartz crystals closely packed together, possibly with some common opal "cement." The crystals are so small that even a microscope cannot reveal their boundaries. But optical means show they are arranged in bands or in radial or sheaf-like groups. The mineral is formed by deposition from a silica-rich solution and forms masses with a nodular surface or stalactites and stalagmites. Some fills veins or cavities in rocks. Agate, which is usually banded, is generally found filling almond-shaped vesicles in rocks.

The term chalcedony, an old name of uncertain origin, is usually applied to non-banded or weakly banded material of a grayish-white hue. Other colors of unbanded chalcedony are usually given their own special names—cornelian for brownish-red chalcedony, sard for the more yellowish-red stones and chrysoprase for green chalcedony. A grayish chalcedony with cloudy patches is sometimes known as cloud chalcedony.

As sealing wax does not readily adhere to polished agate, these stones were widely used as seal stones when sealing wax was a vogue. Much grayish or brownish chalcedony, which at best is only translucent, is carved into small figurines and other small ornamental objects. China and West Germany are the main centers for this kind of work.

A beautiful blue chalcedony is found in South-West Africa and similar material is obtained from the Barstow district of southern California. These blue chalcedonies do not seem to be used in jewelry as much as their attractive color would lead one to expect, but much blue chalcedony is now treated by the tumbling process to fashion baroque stones. Some bluish-white chalcedony has a schiller, somewhat like poor quality moonstone, and has been given the name moonstone with various prefixes.

Chrysoprase

Varying in color from a good apple-green to a less attractive yellowish green, chrysoprase in its best color is the most prized of chalcedonies and has been mistaken for the famed Imperial jade. The stone owes its color to a trace of nickel compound and in earlier days was found in Silesia, a source now said to be exhausted. Material now comes from America or Australia. A bright green chalcedony resembling chrysoprase was found in Rhodesia in 1955, but the coloring agent here is chromium, so the stone cannot truthfully be called chrysoprase. This chrome chalcedony has been given the name of mtorodite. Chrysoprase is cut in the cabochon style. In Victorian times, when the stones were

Many gem minerals were formed in pockets in certain, usually remote, places on earth where conditions were favorable millions of years ago. Sometimes the pockets contain large gem crystals and at others small ones or none at all. That is why gem mining is a hazardous occupation. This is an agate geode which is decorative and useful for making "massive" pieces such as ashtrays but has no fine crystals suitable for cutting as gems.

fairly popular, they were cut into low-domed cabochons with a narrow set of facets around the edge.

Agate

The term agate is usually applied to chalcedony which shows definite bands, colored patterns or layers and may be defined as a variegated chalcedony. The name agate is often used indiscriminately for either banded or unbanded chalcedony.

The cause of banding in agate is not really understood, though various suggestions have been put forward. One is that the nodules have inlets where silica-rich solutions can enter and leave. This solution, flowing intermittently, deposits layers of chalcedony varying somewhat in the impurities that color them. Another theory,

attributed to Dr. Liesegang, is that the banding is caused by rhythmic precipitation of a colored chemical compound which diffuses through the still-liquid silica gel, producing colored bands at intervals. It is possible that there is truth in both theories and that both phenomena occur.

When an agate nodule is cut open, it may show zig-zag bands like the outline of old fortifications. Such a stone is known as fortification agate. When the bands are curved rather than angular it is called topographical agate. Sometimes the bands run straight across the nodule. One type of straight-banded agate has its parallel layers marked with black protuberances. When correctly cut, a scenic effect is produced, which has earned it the name landscape agate.

Agate nodules are found in many parts of the world, but the prime producer is Brazil. North America provides much attractive agate, and Scottish agates are well known. The nodules found in the hills around the Nahe River, which enters the mighty Rhine at Bingen, Germany, supplied the agate originally used by the stone cutters of the twin town of Idar-Oberstein. This source is now exhausted so the agate still cut in quantity there is imported from Brazil.

Moss Agates

The inclusion of other minerals in chalcedony and agate produces a number of interesting variants. Probably the most important of them

One of the world's big gem cutting and dealing centers is Idar-Oberstein in Germany. Much of it is still a home industry where gems are bought in their special folded papers and recorded in the family ledger. This procedure is common in the world of gems.

are those known as moss agates. These stones are usually plain or very weakly banded chalcedony in which the inclusions take the form of tree-like shapes. These dendritic inclusions, as they are called, may be black and formed by a compound of manganese, or green, when the mineral responsible is chlorite.

Besides the green and black inclusions in moss agate, red, yellow and brown are found, caused by iron compounds. Indeed, some attractive moss agates contain moss of two colors. These may be green and red, black and red or brown, or a combination of all. The term mocha stone is sometimes used for moss agate, in particular where there is a brownish moss on a clear creamy-white background. This older name is now less often used.

The cause of these dendritic inclusions is a matter of conjecture. If one accepts the gel theory of the deposition of agate, the mineral could percolate in tree-like shapes before the mass solidifies, or the gel may leave minute cracks when it solidifies, which are later filled by secondary, percolating, silica-bearing solution carrying the colored mineral as an impurity. Otherwise the colored mineral alone may enter the cracks and be deposited in tree-like shapes. A third notion suggests that the chalcedony is built up layer by layer. The tree-like formations could then have been deposited on the surface and covered by later deposits of chalcedony.

India is the main source of green moss agate, but much agate with variously colored moss is found in several states, particularly Montana and Wyoming. Some green moss is also found in agate from Scotland.

Other Agates

Like rock crystal, agate can enclose other minerals. When it does, some interesting agates are formed. The well-known bloodstone, sometimes known as heliotrope, is agate containing masses of antinolite fibers. The red spots are due to the inclusion of an iron mineral. Radiating needle-like groups of natrolite or mordenite are also sometimes seen in agate. Such stones are called sagenitic agates, found in quantity in the United States.

An agate is found in a number of western states, which is colored completely or in cloudy streaks by the bright red mercuric mineral called cinnabar. It is cut in cabochons. These stones have been called myrickite, as cinnabar chalcedony was first found by a Nevada prospector named "Shady" Myrick.

A most unusual type of agate nodule is the so-called thunder egg. These are found in disintegrated rhyolite rock, which often contains gas cavities. These cavities later filled with a kind of mud, which on drying out formed a star-like central cavity. Subsequently, flows of silica-rich water deposited agate in the mud and hardened it and also filled the star-like cavity itself. These thunder eggs, a name derived from an old legend of the American Indians of the West, are found mainly in Oregon and California.

A material which makes an unusual and attractive ornamental stone is brecciated agate, sometimes called ruin agate. This consists of angular fragments of banded agate in a state of disorder, which have been recemented into a solid mass by infiltration of secondary silica. Another interesting type of agate, of no importance as a gemstone, is iris agate. This material is chalcedony whose layers are extremely fine, numbering as many as 12,000 to 20,000 to the inch. They act like a diffraction grating and split up a beam of white light into the spectrum of colors.

Organic substances may be petrified by chalcedony and these pseudomorphs, as they are called, are sometimes cut for ornamental purposes. The most common of these is fossilized wood. This agate consists of tree trunks or branches which have been turned into agate by mineralized water. The wood is replaced by silica, particle by particle, in such a way that the original structure of the wood, though not its composition, remains. The medullary rays running from the center of the tree trunk, which cross the annual rings of growth, are often faithfully preserved in this agatized wood. Much of the coral from Tampa Bay in Florida has been changed to agate, and this fossil coral has been fashioned into cabochons and into baroque shapes by the tumbling process.

Stained Chalcedony

Due to the minute interstices between the crystallites, chalcedony is porous. This porosity, which may vary in the different layers of banded agates, permits the material to be artificially colored. Practically all commercial agate is stained, or altered in color by some means. For instance, natural cornelian is too pale to be attractive, so this nearly colorless or pale brown material is heated in ovens and changed to a much better color by oxidizing the iron content of the stone.

Two distinct methods are used to dye chalcedony. The first is to use aniline dyes. Though bright colors are produced in such dyed agate, they tend to fade rapidly, so the much more stable chemical precipitation method is preferable. The chalcedony is first soaked for some time usually in a hot solution of a chemical, then in another chemical solution which reacts with the first to produce a colored chemical precipitate. This fills the interstices between the crystallites and colors the stone. Black, the so-called black onyx, is made by using a sugar solution followed by a sulphuric acid. The resultant precipitate is black carbon, like soot. A solution of one of the ferrocyanides followed by a solution of iron sulphate produces blue colors by forming a precipitate of Prussian blue.

Red and green are produced by soaking the chalcedony in solutions of iron nitrate (for red) or ammonium bichromate (for green) and then strongly heating the stone. The green stones may closely resemble the better green jadeite, or even emerald. Some care must be taken if a Chelsea color filter is used, for the green-stained chalcedony will also show a red tint through the filter. Some yellow chalcedony is said to be produced by using hydrochloric acid alone, and some unusual colors are produced by other chemicals. These include an attractive pink shade, generally called carneol. An imitation turquoise is also made of stained chalcedony. The dif-

Cameo cutting and polishing needs a well developed artistic ability as well as skill. Italy is the center for shell cameos. The illustration shows the stone cameos being worked on in Idar-Oberstein, Germany. Among stones often used to make cameos are amethyst, agate, onyx and jasper.

ferential porosity of the bands in banded agate will have the effect of emphasizing them, particularly when they are black and white.

Jasper

The impure and heavily pigmented massive quartz known as jasper must be mentioned, for with the varied and colorful patterns it displays, jasper has much to offer as an ornamental stone. Its red, brown, green, bluish and black hues are mostly due to iron compounds or iron-rich clays. The stone may contain as much as 20 per cent of these impurities.

Many names are given to jasper of different colors and patterns. Egyptian jasper is yellowish brown. Ribbon jaspers consist of bands of red and white or red and green, much of the latter being found in the Ural Mountains of Russia. The orbicular jaspers are distinguished by having circular areas of different colors and are common in the western United States. Jaspillite is a jasper interleaved with bands of iron oxide, and this seemingly unlikely material is cut and polished. The so-called jaspagate, or agate jasper, is, as its name implies, a mixture of jasper and true agate. It is used mainly in America. Broken pieces of jasper can be cemented together again to produce brecciated jasper, and rolled pebbles can be cemented together instead of angular fragments to give the rock known as a conglomerate. Hertfordshire pudding stone, a material which has been fashioned into small ornaments, is an example of this.

Wood petrified by replacement with colorful jasper is quite common and some wonderful examples are found in the famous petrified forest of Arizona. Jasperized wood is quite commonly cut and polished for ornaments, particularly in the United States. An unusual material that has been used for small worked objects, such as small carved tortoises, is the fossil dinosaur bone found in Wyoming, Colorado and Utah. The agatized bones of these gigantic extinct reptiles still show its bony structure. This material is sometimes called "dinny bone."

Though too colorful a material to need staining, jasper is, however, stained blue by chemical precipitation to produce an imitation lapis lazuli, though another form of impure quartz, called chert is often used. This blue-dyed jasper is marketed under the name Swiss lapis, though its color is never as rich as that of true lapis lazuli, nor does it show the brassy specks of iron pyrites so common in the real stone.

14. Turquoise

TURQUOISE was certainly known as early as 3,000 B.C. In fact, there is evidence to suggest that it was used as early as, and even before, the First Egyptian Dynasty, for bracelets found on the mummy of Queen Zer are said to be set with alternate plaques of cast gold and carved turquoise. In prehistoric times, when ancient peoples prized the minerals found in the earth for their color alone, the beautiful blue or greenish-blue of turquoise must have made it one of the earliest materials to be used.

The ancient names for turquoise were callais and callaite. They probably referred to the true turquoise, though some authorities question this. The early Persians knew turquoise under the general name smaragdus, a word in common use at that time for any green stone. The derivation of the name turquoise is obscure and there is much confusion over it. Coming from the old French *tourques*, it is thought to be just a corruption of the French name for Turkish. This is not because the stone was found in Turkey, but because the best turquoise, probably imported by the Venetians, came through Turkey from the East.

Alternatively, it is claimed that the name was derived from the Persian word *piruzeh*, of which there are several transliterations. Though it is difficult to connect this word with our present name turquoise, many claim this is the true derivation. In early Chinese literature turquoise was referred to as *tien-tse*, but the more modern names are *lu sung-shi* and *sung-tse shi*, meaning green fir tree and fir-cone stone respectively. The ancient Aztecs called the stone *chalcihuitl*,

but this name was given by them to many green minerals.

A stone with such a long history abounds with lore and superstition. It is said that turquoise should be given and not bought, as it will then remove any animosity between the parties concerned. Its hue is said to indicate the state of the wearer's health, and its luster to tell if any peril awaits him. Turquoise is also said to arouse sexual passion and was once supposed to betray the infidelity of a wife by changing color. In olden days it was the horseman's talisman, for it was said that "so long as the rider hath the turquoise with him, his horse will never tire, and it will preserve him in any accident and defend him that carries it from untoward and evil casualties." The Apache tribe of Indians called the turquoise by the name *duklij* and supposed the stone helped the warrior and hunter by ensuring the accuracy of his aim.

Turquoise occurs in the Old World in Iran and Egypt. It is also said to be the national stone of Tibet, though its occurrence in that country has not been confirmed. In Tibet the most highly prized color is green and green turquoise is known there as *gyu*, pronounced "yu," a name given to jade in China. Turquoise does not seem to have been known to the peoples of old China and India before the 14th century, when the stone was probably introduced by the Mogul invaders, who called it *kiris*. It is doubtful whether turquoise is indigenous to either of these countries, though there may be deposits in China. Turquoise occurs in many other places throughout the world, usually in desert or arid regions, but only those in the New World are of any importance.

Egyptian Turquoise

Undoubtedly the turquoise used by the Egyptians over 4,000 years ago came from the Sinai Peninsula, a source of scant importance today. The deposits there lie in a range of mountains bordering the peninsula's south-western coastline and stretch over some 250 square miles (650 sq. km.) south of the sandy desert of Debbet el Qeri (or Ramleh). The country is rugged and bare and is remarkable for the extensive faulting of the highly eroded sedimentary and igneous rocks. This produces canyon-like valleys or *wadis*, which are turned into raging torrents after a few minutes of heavy rain.

The most important of the six turquoise mines is that of Wadi Maghareh, which means "the valley of the cave or grotto," and is the site of extremely ancient workings. Although some sporadic mining has been carried out in recent times, only a few destitute Bedouins search for turquoise today, and even they only search the old mine dumps. Other ancient mines are Sarabit el Khadim, Um Bogma, Abu Hamed and Wadi Shellal.

Sinai turquoise is thought to have been formed by meteoric waters, bearing in solution carbon dioxide and sulfur derived from organic matter existing on the basalts. This water decomposed some of the soluble parts of the volcanic rock. Since any rock decomposed by the more soluble bases, to give a concentration of the relatively more insoluble oxides of iron, aluminum and silica, some of these minerals were carried down in suspension or in solution. As these waters descended, other constituents in the sandstone and limestone, such as phosphorus, carbonaceous matter from fossil remains and copper, which is also known to exist in the shales and plant remains, were also carried down.

After passing through fissures in the top strata, the waters descended further into the underlying sandstone until they became super-saturated and formed a zone of cementation. Earth movements then exerted pressure on them and caused them to harden, dry and become concentrated until the turquoise is formed.

Egyptian turquoise is blue to pale green, often with white spots. It is moderately translucent, but commonly includes small patches of sandstone. The Bedouins have a trick of enhancing the color by soaking the stones in oil and polishing them with an oily rag. Local lapidaries have been known to paint the stones.

Iranian Turquoise

The most beautiful turquoise comes from Iran, which, as far as turquoise is concerned, is better known under its old name of Persia. The most important mines are in the mountains around Nishapur, which lies some 15 miles (24 km.) west of the town of Meshed, now called Mashhad, in the province of Khorasan. The turquoise fills cracks and crevices in the trachyte rock which forms the breccia on the southern slopes of the peak called Ali-mersai. The turquoise is said to have been formed by the decomposition of the feldspar crystals, and is often found in the shape of these crystals. But most turquoise is found as small irregular pieces distributed throughout the rock or collected together in plate-like masses in limonite, which, being an earlier mineral than the turquoise, tends to line the cavities.

Turquoise is also found at the foot of the mountain in the debris formed by the weathering of the rock masses. The turquoise found lying loose in the debris usually have a white crust which needs removing before the lovely blue turquoise is revealed. Many of the mines at Nishapur have been abandoned, but a few are still being worked. Persian turquoise is usually a fine dark blue, but pale or greenish stones are also found. The greenish stones are often more coveted in some parts of the East than the fine blue stones so prized in the West. The village of Maaden, which lies in a valley some 5,100 feet (1,530 meters) above sea level, is the turquoise cutting and marketing center.

The Aztecs

The Aztec Indians were using turquoise when Cortez conquered Mexico, and some of the turquoise mosaics the Spanish conquerors brought back testified to the skill and taste of the Indian artisans. The Aztecs called the finest and most attractive turquoise *teuxivitl*, a name which signified turquoise of the gods. The stone was said to be very rare and to have been brought to Mexico from afar. The stone was exclusively devoted to the service of the gods and the decoration of divine images and nobody was allowed to wear it.

Where the Aztecs obtained their turquoise is not definitely known, for little turquoise is found in Mexico. True, some turquoise has been found in Lower California, Zacatecas and Sonora, and there is a deposit of turquoise at the Chugincamata mine in northern Chile, where the material is said to be equal in color to the Persian turquoise. It is more likely that the turquoise the Aztecs used came from the area north of Mexico, which now forms the southwestern states of Nevada, New Mexico and Arizona. California should perhaps be included.

The Southwest

Turquoise was extensively used in aboriginal times for beads, pendants and earrings, and for mosaics, by the Pueblo people of the American Southwest, but strangely they did not seem to have embellished their silver work with turquoise until about late in the 19th century. The existence of ancient workings on Mount Chalchihuitl in the Cerrillos Hills of New Mexico

has led to the idea that this was the source of the Aztecs' turquoise, and probably of the Toltecs' before them. Finding that these aboriginal Indians of New Mexico inlaid turquoise as the Aztecs did adds weight to this idea.

Turquoise, usually pale in color and soft and chalky, is found in the Globe-Miami district of Gila County, Arizona. Much of it is made more usable by a recent method of bonding the friable material in plastics. Other localities in Arizona produce more compact turquoise of a finer blue. Nevada is rich in turquoise and a number of mines are worked there. A mine at Battle Mountain in Lander County, worked by tunnels, produced a nugget of turquoise weighing 178 lbs.

The turquoise found in San Bernardino County, California, has little commercial importance, but is of great historical interest. Much has been written about it of archeological value. It has been found that the California turquoise mines were worked by the Pueblo people from Arizona and New Mexico, who probably entered the area and worked the mines each season. They worked exposed turquoise veins in open pits, breaking the rock with hafted stone axes and hammers. They excavated the broken rock with scoops made from the carapaces of turtles or the shoulder blades of other animals. Colorado is another state with many turquoise mines, though their commercial importance does not seem to be great.

Properties of Turquoise

Turquoise varies in color from nearly white, through pale blue to a rich sky-blue. The color of a perfect stone is robin's-egg blue. The stone's blue color is ascribed to copper, while the presence of iron or zinc in it gives it a greenish hue. The copper may well be present as copper phosphate or aluminate, but one theory suggests it could be a complex amino copper ion, that has come from organic remains. This might also account for turquoise turning green, as sometimes happens, possibly by hydration. Some American turquoise fades more readily than the material from the Orient.

Despite its softness compared with other gems, turquoise can take a good polish, and any scratches on its surface are less noticeable than on transparent faceted stones. Turquoise is rarely faceted, the cabochon with various outlines being the most commonly used style of cutting. Much turquoise is carved, and polished flat plates are used for inlay. Large flattish plates of turquoise, often with a backing of limonite, come from the East engraved with quotations from the Koran. The incised letters and ornamental border are often inlaid with gold or silver. They are largely used as charms and amulets, as superstition credits the stone with bringing the wearer good luck. The Moslem tries to ensure this by adding quotations from his own sacred book.

Nodular masses of turquoise often exhibit fine limonite veins like spider's webs, and much turquoise is disseminated throughout brecciated rock in pieces too small to be cut into useful stones. The turquoise and the matrix of dark brown limonite or fawn-colored sandstone are then cut together to give stones known as turquoise matrix or, if the veins are fine, spider-web turquoise.

As turquoise is porous, a feature usually more marked in American material than in that from the East, it needs care. Cosmetics, perspiration, detergents and household chemicals can have a harmful effect on it, making its beautiful blue color dingy. But another consequence is that the stones respond to beauty treatment. Much turquoise is waxed—treated with paraffin wax—which can brighten or darken the color. There is a danger, however, that the wax may deteriorate with age. Porous American turquoise is often bonded in plastic or even silica glass to make it more compact and much of this bonded turquoise is marketed.

Simulants

Certain natural minerals which resemble turquoise deserve a mention. Variscite is one, though it is usually much greener than turquoise. This mineral was first found in nodules in Utah and at one time was called utahlite, while that found near Lucin was named lucinite. Neither of these names is used today. There are other American sources of variscite. Material from the vicinity of Dayboro in Queensland, Australia, was at one time put out as Australian turquoise or Australian jade, though it is distinct from both turquoise and jade. Chrysocolla is another mineral which can simulate turquoise. The Eilat stone from Israel may contain turquoise as well as many other copper minerals like chrysocolla.

One of the most fascinating imitations of turquoise is odontolite, which is variously known as bone turquoise, tooth turquoise, fossil turquoise and turquoise *de la nouvelle roche*. Odontolite is not strictly a mineral, but is really fossil ivory or bone, being the teeth and bones of extinct vertebrates, which have been impregnated with the blue mineral vivianite as they became fossilized. When taken out of the ground, odontolite is a dingy grayish-blue. The fine blue color is not produced until after the stone has been moderately heated. Odontolite is found in the Miocene beds of Simorre, near Auch in southern France. Another simulant of turquoise is the blue-dyed howlite, a compact white mineral found as nodules in California.

Artificially produced simulants of turquoise are too numerous to mention individually. Most are made by pressing chemical precipitates of similar composition to turquoise into a solid mass. A synthetic turquoise has been made by a French firm, but there seems little fear that it cannot be detected by a trained gemmologist.

Chalcedony stained a turquoise color makes a fair imitation, but is not at all common. Another rarity is suitably stained bone.

Even in pre-dynastic times of ancient Egypt, faïence, a glazed siliceous ware, was made in a blue color, perhaps to imitate turquoise. Egypt is usually accorded the honor of inventing glass, too, but these early glasses were generally opaque, rarely transparent, and always colored. Copper compounds were used to tint the early Egyptian blue glass. Copper and copper oxides are the usual coloring agents for paste turquoise made today. They can usually be identified with a hand lens, which reveals small gas bubbles just beneath the surface.

Birthstones

MONTH	COLOR	OFFICIAL STONE	ALTERNATIVE
January	dark red	garnet	
February	purple	amethyst	
March	pale blue	aquamarine	bloodstone
April	white (transparent)	diamond	rock crystal
May	bright green	emerald	chrysoprase
June	cream	pearl	moonstone
July	red	ruby	cornelian
August	pale green	peridot	sardonyx
September	deep blue	sapphire	lapis lazuli
October	variegated	opal	
November	yellow	topaz or golden quartz	
December	sky blue	turquoise	

15. Jade

JADE IS PRIZED by peoples the world over and had a profound significance, religious and secular, in many ancient civilizations. Jade is so often green that jade-green has become a household expression. Yet jade is not always green.

The name jade may be correctly applied to two different minerals, which the mineralogist calls nephrite and jadeite. The early Chinese called the jade from which they made such beautiful carvings *yu*. This was nephrite, but the so-called Chinese jade of the present day is jadeite, a type of jade that did not enter China until the 18th century. Of the two jades, jadeite is more highly prized as a mineral. The great value of the older Chinese nephrite carvings lies in their antiquity and beauty of craftsmanship.

The name jade is derived from the Spanish (*piedra de la*) *ijada*, which means kidney stone and is latinized as *lapis nephriticus*, which gives us the name nephrite.

Nephrite is the oldest known form of jade and is most commonly dark green or leek green. But there are grayish-green and greenish-white nephrites, the latter usually known as mutton-fat jade. Some nephrite can be brown, if its iron content has been oxidized. Many boulders, cobbles and pebbles of nephrite have their outside skin weathered to a brown shade and the Chinese carvers take advantage of this to give their carvings a two-color effect.

Nephrite

Nephrite is composed of a mass of interlocking fibrous crystals of actinolite or tremolite, which give jade its toughness. The nephrite used by the early Chinese carvers probably came from the Kuen Lun Mountains of eastern Turkestan and from boulders found in the beds of the Yurungkash, Karakash and Keriya Rivers, which drain these mountains. In 1850, large boulders of black-spotted dark green nephrite were found in the rivers which run into Lake Baikal, to the south of Irkutsk in southern Siberia. These boulders are thought to have originated in the Sayan Mountains of Mongolia.

The nephrite jade found in the Southern Alps of New Zealand was fashioned by the Maoris into neck ornaments in the form of grotesque human figures, which they call *hei tiki* and *meres*—flattened clubs. The Maoris called this jade *pounamu*, but it is known in the West as Maori stone, New Zealand jade, New Zealand greenstone, or sometimes, from its use as early axeheads, axestone. This stone is not only found in the Griffin Range of mountains, but also as flattened pebbles in the rivers and streams that run down from them. The flattened pieces are of a more convenient shape for fashioning into meres.

The discovery of nephrite jade at Jordanov in Silesia, a part of Poland, aroused speculation that this could be the source of the nephrite artifacts found in the Swiss lake dwellings. Nephrite is found elsewhere in Silesia too, some of it creamy-white or sandy, splashed with green patches.

Much of the jade used by the Incas of Peru and the Aztecs of Mexico was jadeite, but some was nephrite, of which alluvial deposits have been found in Mexico. These may well be the source of the jade used by these ancient American civilizations. The nephrite jade in the Amazon Valley is thought to have been worked by native Indians of an earlier period. Many nephrite artifacts found at Amargoza in Bahia date from this early period.

Nephrite is found in various places in North America. That found around Lander in Wyoming is probably the best known. It occurs in water-borne boulders and angular blocks, varying in size from small pebbles and cobbles to large pieces weighing up to four tons. The Wyoming nephrite jade varies from green to black, the latter probably a very dark green. The so-called Wyoming jade or snowflake jade, a rock-like mixture of nephrite and albite feldspar, also appears to come from this locality.

Chinese miners panning for gold along the rivers in Placer County, California, recovered many alluvial boulders of nephrite jade. It is thought this material was taken to China and carved into various objects. Nephrite pebbles are also found along the coast of Monterey County, California. There is said to be a deposit of nephrite in San Luis Obispo County in the same state.

Some 150 miles (240 km.) from the mouth of the Kobuk River in northwestern Alaska lies Jade Mountain, a source of nephrite jade. Boulders of this material are also found in the Kobuk and Noatak Rivers. The small amount of jade recovered from this Arctic area is flown out by aircraft. In British Columbia, alluvial boulders of nephrite have been recovered from the Upper Lewis and Frazer Rivers, and much of this material is now marketed. In the 1950's, a deposit of nephrite jade was found in the Mashaba district of Rhodesia, of a dark spinach-green color, marked with black specks which may be inclusions of chromite, a common mineral there. Nephrite has also recently been found in Taiwan. A black nephrite comes from Australia.

Jadeite

Unlike nephrite, whose color range is restricted to greenish-white and dark greens, or brown on the weathered parts, the more highly prized jadeite can be found in many different colors, from pure white through red, orange, brown, mauve, blue and violet to black. The most highly prized is a highly translucent rich emerald green, called Imperial green jade. Much jadeite is mottled green and white. Green is more commonly mottled than the other colors, which are not normally mottled, except, perhaps, for mauve (mottled with green). There is also a black or very dark green jadeite called chloromelanite, but this is rare. If it is met with, the name jadeite will suffice for it. The toughness of jadeite is again due to its interlocking crystals, though these are more granular than the fibrous crystals which form nephrite.

It is not known for sure how the jadeite deposits came to be discovered in a remote and unhealthy part of Burma. The mineral was of little interest to the local natives, but became esteemed by the neighboring Chinese, who considered that it surpassed in beauty and value anything that they possessed.

Though there is no supporting evidence in Chinese writings, it has been suggested that Burmese jadeite first reached China during the 13th century. The story goes that the discovery of fine quality green jade in northern Burma was made accidentally by a trader from the Chinese province of Yunnan. While returning from a journey across the frontier, he is said to have picked up a piece of stone to balance the load on his mule. On returning to China he found that his balance weight was jade of great value. A large party returned to procure more of this jade, but nobody was able to tell them where the stone could be found so the endeavor was unsuccessful.

In the 14th century, the Yunnan government

Jade is found in the form of boulders. In this picture a portable saw is being used to make a test cut on a boulder found along Bridge River in British Columbia to assess its value.

made another attempt to find the source of the jade, but this also failed. All the members of the expedition are said to have perished, either from disease or at the hands of the hill tribes. Though small pieces of stone occasionally found their way across the frontier, no further attempt was made to seek it out. Not until 1769, when a written contract ended hostilities between China and Burma, did a regular trade in the mineral develop. It was taken to Canton for cutting and polishing.

Jadeite is mined at Tawmaw, on a plateau between the Chindwin and Irrawaddy Rivers, about 70 miles (112 km.) north-west of Mogaung and a similar distance from Myitkyina. The stone is found in dikes of igneous rock and as boulders in the local streams and is mined by primitive methods. The blocks of jadeite sold to Chinese buyers are mawed before sale—that is, a polished flat surface about 1 by 1$\frac{1}{2}$ in. (2.5 by 3.75 cm.) is ground on them to give an idea of their color. But this may not be typical, as the color is often not uniform throughout the stone.

Most of the jades of ancient Mexico were jadeite. Where then did this material originate? It is thought to have come from Mexico itself or from Guatemala. The Aztecs and Mayas of old Mexico called the jadeite which they valued so highly and worked so elaborately *quetzal chalchihuitl*, as it resembled the gorgeous metallic-green plumage of the quetzal bird. By a strange coincidence, the Chinese called the brilliant green jade by the name *feits' ui*, which is derived from the name of the kingfisher, another bird.

In the mid-1930's, a deposit of jadeite was found in San Benito County, California. Since then further deposits have been recorded in other parts of that state. One of the more interesting is found at Leach Lake Mountain. It is sawn into slabs and exported to the German cutters. It is not a true jade but a mixture of nephrite and jadeite, though it can still be called by the name jade. California jades do not display the beauty or translucency of Burmese jade, nor its color, since they vary from a dark grayish-green to bluish-green. They are usually more or less opaque. There have been unconfirmed reports of jadeite occurring in China and Tibet and also in Japan.

It is sometimes difficult to distinguish true jadeite from certain other rocks, such as that found near Namshamaw in Upper Burma. First called maw-sit-sit, from the name of the village where it was found, the rock was found to be a mixture of chrome-rich jadeite and albite feldspar, so the name jade albite has been proposed for it. Another material called smaragdite, which is opaque and brilliant emerald green and black, may be a form of chloromelanite or even maw-sit-sit.

Simulants

As jadeite is composed of interlocking crystals it is slightly porous. Advantage has been taken of this to alter its color by dyeing. An Imperial jade color is introduced into white jadeite by using a combination of two organic dyes, one blue and the other yellow. Dyed material has been marketed, but the dyestuffs tend to fade, sometimes quite rapidly. A hand lens will usually show the dyestuff outlining the crystal grains. White jadeite is also dyed mauve. It is usually too intense a shade to pass for the rather pale mauve of natural mauve jadeite. The mauve-dyed jadeite does not seem to fade like the green-dyed jadeite.

Another jadeite fake is the jade triplet, a composite stone made in three pieces. A central cabochon of white jadeite forms the core of the stone. It is covered by a hollow cabochon of similar material, while a third piece forms the back cover. The three pieces are cemented together with a green cement which gives the stone an excellent green color. These composite stones are obvious for what they are when unset, but when the join is concealed by the setting, they can be very deceptive. As far as is known these triplets do not fade, so a different coloring agent must be used.

The imitation of jade by other minerals of similar appearance must next be considered. The most important imitation of jade today is the bowenite form of serpentine. A harder form of it varies from a pale yellowish green to a dark green, usually with cloudy inclusions. Much of this kind of serpentine comes from China as carved figurines and is often sold as "new jade," a name which is illegal in England. Bowenite is found in Kashmir, China and New Zealand, the latter providing beautiful translucent dark green material, which was worked by the Maoris, who called it *tangiwaite*.

A much softer serpentine, still of jade color, is found high up in the Karakoram Mountains in Kashmir. Bowenite serpentine, while harder than the other forms of this mineral, is hard enough not to be easily scratched with the blade of a knife, though it can be so marked, a fact which distinguishes it from true jade.

Often mentioned as a jade simulant is saussurite, a rock-like mixture of zoisite and albite feldspar. Seemingly it had little importance and was rarely encountered, but recently a number of carvings have appeared which have a whitish ground with patches of green. This saussurite has a great similarity to some jades and is distinguished from them with difficulty.

An apprentice jade carver today. Many jade sculptures though 3,000 or more years old are astonishingly "modern" in form. Today there are jade studios in Peking, Shanghai, Tientsin, Canton, Yangchow and Chinchow; in the Peking studios alone there are more than 1,500 craftsmen.

A number of jade-colored carvings have been marketed in recent years, made of natural or dyed soapstone. Soapstone, which is very soft, has been used for countless years for Chinese carvings under the name agalmatolite or figure stone, though another mineral, a massive alteration product of pinite, is often given this name. Much green soapstone is used by native carvers in eastern Africa, and a similar gray-green material is used by the Eskimos of northern Canada.

A massive grossular garnet, mineralogically a hydrogrossular, as it contains some water in chemical combination, is found in the Transvaal and elsewhere. It is an important jade simulant and often contains black specks of chromite, a further resemblance to nephrite from Rhodesia and Lake Baikal. The massive type of mineral idocrase called californite also has a jade-like appearance. These two minerals commonly intermix to produce a jade-colored rock now used for carved and polished objects. This poses a problem in nomenclature.

Green aventurine quartz, sometimes miscalled Indian jade, chrysoprase, green chalcedony and bluish-green smithsonite are other minerals some specimens of which can resemble jade. There is also a soft variety of serpentine found in Burgenland in Austria, which has been given the name pseudophite. This is misnamed Styrian jade and, though somewhat opaque, attractive thin-walled bowls and other objects have been carved from it. Lastly, verdite, an opaque brilliant green rock, often with yellow or red spots, deserves mention, though its resemblance to jade is weak. It is found in the Transvaal and one or two other places in the world.

The uninitiated may confuse Connemara marble, a serpentinous marble, with jade. But it is easy to detect, for a spot of acid placed on its surface will fizz. This is also true of smithsonite. Suitably colored and opacified glass is made to imitate jade, but such pieces are obvious by their glassy luster and by the small bubbles they contain, which can usually be seen with a hand lens. Jade has also been successfully imitated, as far as appearance goes, by some plastics, but their very lightness when held in the hand, as well as the ease with which they can be marked with a knife blade, makes them only too obvious. Jade probably has more simulants than any other stone in fact, apart, perhaps, from turquoise.

89

16. Ornamental Stones

LET US NOW TURN to the stones which, while sometimes used as gemstones are more often used for small objects and contrasting inlays. First is malachite, a beautiful green mineral used as an ornamental stone, but also as a jewel stone and for beads. This mineral, of which good pieces suitable for ornamental uses are becoming rare, is formed from the solution of copper ores. It is deposited in fissures and cavities in rocks or as stalagmites. Owing to the radial arrangement of the many crystallites which form its compact mass, it may resemble banded agate, though malachite is always green and the bands in different shades of the same color.

The most important sources of malachite are the world's great copper belts. At one time, probably the most important source of massive malachite was Nizhe-Tagilsk in Siberia, where blocks weighing several tons were discovered. This material was extensively used by the lapidaries of imperial Russia. The most important source of malachite today is the Katanga district of Zaïre, though much workable material is also found at Burra Burra, South Australia. Fair quality malachite is found in Arizona too, but that found in other parts of the world is unsuitable for artistic uses.

Polished pieces of malachite, banded with another copper carbonate mineral, dark blue azurite, are sometimes met with. This combination of two minerals, banded in green and blue, goes by the name azurmalachite. A rock-like ornamental stone, consisting of a mixture of malachite, turquoise and other copper minerals, is found near Eilat in Israel, at the site of the so-called King's Solomon's mines and sold as Eilat stone.

Lapis Lazuli

Lapis lazuli, which is highly esteemed for ornamentation and for objets d'art, is of ancient origin. It is eminently suitable for seal stones in rings, for beads to be strung as necklaces, for small boxes and vases, and as polished pieces for inlay work. The name is a medieval Latin form of the Persian *lazhward*, which signifies the sky and was later applied to anything blue. It is not known when the name lapis lazuli was first applied to this blue stone. In olden times it was called sapphirus, the modern version of which is sapphire, the highly prized blue corundum.

Lapis lazuli is actually a rock, not a single mineral. It consists of an aggregate of several distinct minerals—hauynite, mainly responsible for the beautiful blue of lapis lazuli, sodalite, another blue mineral of which more will be said later in this chapter, noselite and lazurite, the latter possibly a combination of hauynite and sodalite. Calcium carbonate in the form of calcite is always present. Bright brassy specks of pyrites are often seen in lapis lazuli too, and are taken as a sign that the stone is genuine. Lapis lazuli is formed in the earth by metamorphosis. Heat and pressure by masses of molten granite intrude on an impure limestone and alter it to marble. Lapis lazuli and other minerals then separate out.

The best known source of lapis lazuli, said to have been known and intermittently worked for 6,000 years, lies in the Badakshan district of mountainous northeastern Afghanistan. The

The blue and gold mineral lapis-lazuli is used for the ends of these bullet-shaped cuff links in gold and diamonds, designed by Yoshira Mochizuki of Japan.

lapis lazuli here occurs in a black and white limestone and is the best quality found anywhere. The actual locality is Firgamu, on the upper reaches of the Kokcha River, a tributary of the mighty Oxus. The stone is mined in a primitive manner by heating the rock and then quenching it, so it breaks into blocks weighing about 10 lbs. apiece (4.5 kilos), a size convenient for removal from the rugged terrain. The dark blue of Afghan lapis lazuli may be due to this heating.

There is an abundant deposit of lapis lazuli in the Chilean Andes, but it is pale blue and often tinged with green and disfigured with white patches of calcite. The Chilean deposits lie at the sources of the Vias and Cazadores, tributaries of the Rio Grande, in the Ovalle Cordillera of Coquimbo Province. The rock occurs in blocks of various sizes in a thick bed of white and gray limestone. Weathering produces fragments and pebbles which form local secondary deposits. Near Antofagasta in northern Chile are other deposits.

Near the Mongolian border at the southern end of Lake Baikal lie the Sayan Mountains.

Here a light blue lapis lazuli is found in masses of crystalline limestone. The mines there are said to have ceased working at the end of the 19th century. There has been no authentic news since then. Little use seems to have been made of the deposit of lapis lazuli in the Dataw valley near Mogok in Burma.

The most important source of lapis lazuli in North America is on Italian Mountain in Colorado. Situated some 12,000 feet (3,600 meters) above sea level, the deposit of good-colored material is not sufficiently accessible for its exploitation to be economic. There is another source of lapis lazuli at the junction of the San Bernardino and San Gabriel Mountains, about 40 miles (64 km.) east of Los Angeles, California. The quality of this stone is quite good.

Lapis Simulants

The most common imitation of lapis lazuli is chert, a type of jasper which is tinted blue by the chemical precipitation of Prussian blue, using ferrous sulphate and potassium cyanide. This

91

imitation is known as Swiss lapis. A newer simulant is sintered synthetic spinel, colored blue with cobalt oxide. Said first to have been made by a German dentist, this material is produced by sintering (heating to a point just below the melting point) powdered blue synthetic spinel in an oven. Small specks of gold have sometimes been incorporated in the stones during manufacture to imitate the brassy specks of pyrites so common in genuine lapis lazuli. It is obvious merely on inspection. Glass imitations are made of opacified glass tinted a suitable blue, and sometimes with patches of goldstone—glass which includes copper crystals, put there to imitate pyrites.

The mineral lazulite does not commonly occur, but the deeper colored material bears a good resemblance to lapis lazuli. But probably the mineral that best simulates lapis lazuli is sodalite, itself one of the constituents of lapis lazuli. Found mostly in Canada, sodalite is usually a lighter blue than lapis lazuli and often marked with pink spots, though brassy specks of pyrites are rarely included. In the trade this Canadian material is commonly called Canadian bluestone or just bluestone. Like lapis lazuli it is often used as a contrasting inlay with onyx marbles. Some rich-colored sodalite is found in South-West Africa, but though very beautiful, it is rather coarsely crystalline and tends to shatter more easily than the compact Canadian sodalite.

Rhodochrosite

Another ornamental stone which may resemble malachite by its banding, though not its color, is the rose-red rhodochrosite. This attractive stone, which is sometimes quite translucent and free from banding, is also used for small objects, beads and inlays. It is found in various places around the world, but the best material for ornamental uses comes from San Luís in Argentina. This beautiful material, which first came on the market about 1930, was then marketed as Rosinca and Inca Rose, names derived from the Incas of the Andes. Rhodochrosite is found in the United States, but the only really usable ornamental material occurs near Philipsburg and Butte in Montana, where massive pink opaque rhodochrosite suitable for polishing into cabochons is found.

Rhodonite

Similar in color and rather similar in appearance to rhodochrosite, though it is not banded, is rhodonite which also has a somewhat similar composition. Usually distinguished by its veins and patches of black manganese oxide, rhodonite is found in large masses near Sverdlovsk in the Ural Mountains and is another ornamental stone the jewelers of old Russia often used. Australia is another source of rhodonite and so is North America, where several states have deposits of this glorious pink mineral. It is used less for inlays and more for beads and small objects, such as ashtrays and boxes.

Fluorspar

Fluorspar is another mineral which has been extensively used for carved figures. The massive green type is the most widely used. Figurines carved from green fluorspar may look rather like green beryl, which has also been so used, though fluorspar nearly always shows prominent cleavage cracks. They are easy to distinguish because fluorspar is readily scratched with a knife blade and beryl is not.

The most important form of fluorspar is the banded Blue John or Derbyshire spar, with white-blue, violet, purple or nearly black bands on a nearly white or reddish ground. Treak Cliff, near Castleton in Derbyshire, England, is the only known source, but this mine is now said to be exhausted. Another type of massive fluorspar is Yellow Ashover spar, obtained from the Ashover quarries in Derbyshire. It is bright yellow. Another variety of massive fluorspar is grayish-white or nearly colorless and veined with yellowish-brown markings.

Onyx Marble

Something must be said of the stalagmitic calcites, more commonly known as onyx marbles. These stones are neither onyx, which is properly a form of chalcedony, nor marble. In the ornamental stone trade they are sometimes known by local names, such as Brazilian onyx or Algerian onyx, which are probably not acceptable under present-day law. Onyx marbles form from waters charged with calcium bicarbonate. The loss of the carbon dioxide from this water solution through variations of heat and pressure, eventually causes the calcium carbonate to be precipitated as beds or stalagmites in caverns through which the mineral-charged waters have percolated.

Onyx marble, which is usually white or green and often veined in contrasting colors, is quarried in various places throughout the world. The so-called Brazilian onyx comes from the province of San Luís in Argentina. It is white or green and marked with sinuous veins of dark orange, amber or brown. A similar onyx marble is found in the Pedrara quarries of Lower California, Mexico, and there are other deposits in Mexico proper.

Pakistan also yields a green onyx marble with straight bands of orange-brown. Yava onyx is found in Yavapai County, Arizona, while near Lehi in Utah, is a deposit of lemon-yellow onyx marble. But the richest yellow onyx comes from near Karabib in South-West Africa. Onyx marbles are used for making cigarette boxes, ash trays, clock cases and other small articles, and are often inlaid with other ornamental stones of contrasting color.

Alabaster

Alabaster, a mineral known when the Assyrian and Egyptian cultures were at their height, is used for small objects and carvings. These ancient peoples used alabaster for vases and lamps. It is so soft that it can be scratched with a fingernail and so is eminently suitable for easy working into useful and decorative objects. Attractive dishes, boxes and clock cases are made from it. Alabaster is usually white and often prettily marked with orange and brown veins, but can be of many colors and vary considerably in its degree of translucency. This mineral is the massive form of gypsum (calcium sulphate).

It is usually formed when limestone is acted upon by sulfuric acid derived from iron pyrites. Large alabaster deposits are found in dried-up sea beds and lake basins. Beautiful alabaster is found and worked in Staffordshire and Derbyshire, England. More heavily pigmented material comes from the Volterra district of Tuscany, Italy. It occurs worldwide, however.

Serpentine

The harder form of serpentine has already been discussed as a jade simulant, so let us now concentrate on the more rock-like types of serpentine. A serpentine breccia—small angular pieces of serpentine cemented together by secondary mineralization—constituted the famed Verde Antico of the classical period. But today the best known source and type of serpentine rock is that found at the Lizard in Cornwall, England. Although usually green, serpentine can be brown or reddish brown. Some is marked like the skin of a serpent, which may have been the origin of the name serpentine.

Many types of serpentine are known, coming from many different parts of the world. Apart from bowenite and the rock-like form which every tourist to Cornwall knows, there is williamsite, an emerald-green variety containing small square-shaped crystals. A semi-translucent green variety is found in the Karakoram Mountains of Kashmir. All of these have been used in the arts at some time. Pseudophite, a soft dull green material, which, as has already been mentioned, has been sold under the name Styrian jade, is often classed among the serpentines. So is verdite, a bright green rock with yellow spots, occasionally met as worked pieces or as an inlay. This material comes mainly from South Africa, though other sources are known.

Soapstone

Massive talc, also called steatite, but better known as soapstone, has a very special niche, for being so soft that it can readily be fashioned and carved with a knife blade and finished with a light polishing. For this reason soapstone has endeared itself to native carvers the world over. It varies greatly in color, and may be white, brown, gray and green. Sometimes colored veins increase its attractiveness. A greenish-gray soapstone is used by the Eskimos of Canada for their typical carvings, which are sold to tourists by many stores in the large towns. The natives of eastern Africa use the locally obtainable green soapstone for their tourist carvings.

Meerschaum

To conclude this chapter I must mention meerschaum. Aging to yellow-brown on the surface of polished pieces, this material is well known for its use for the bowls of smoking pipes, many of them elaborately carved with heads. The best of them are collectors' pieces. Meerschaum, or sepiolite to give it its mineralogical name, is found mainly in Asia Minor, but some comes from Spain and the United States. In earlier times the material was found in Morocco and was then used as a substitute for soap.

17. Gems from the Chemist

VARIOUS NAMES have been given to gems made by man to imitate stones of natural origin. Terms such as synthetic, artificial and imitation have been used in different senses by different people. In this volume I shall not use the term artificial. Synthetic, which to the purist means a stone of the same chemical composition and crystal structure as its natural counterpart, will now include those crystalline stones which have no counterpart in nature. Imitation stones will include such materials as glass and the man-made resins usually called plastics. Finally, we must consider composite stones made of two or more parts.

Synthetics

Synthetic crystals are grown in a number of different ways. The main method involves high temperature/high pressure techniques, and has been used to produce synthetic diamonds. But ruby, sapphire and a beautiful range of colors of synthetic spinel, as well as synthetic rutile and strontium titanate, which is better known as Fabulite, are grown as pear-shaped crystals by a flame-fusion process invented by the French chemist A. Verneuil.

In this process, puffs of chemical powder of the right composition are tapped down a stream of oxygen in an inverted oxy-hydrogen blow-pipe. Hydrogen is delivered to the burner by an outer annular tube. The chemical powder melts as it passes through the hot flame and falls onto a ceramic support, where it solidifies and crystallizes to form a pear-shaped mass called a *boule*. The stones are cut from these boules.

The Verneuil method is just one way of growing crystals from a melt. Another is the pulling technique devised by Czochralski. A seed crystal is gently lowered into contact with the surface of the melt, which is of the same composition as the stone. This seed is then gradually drawn upwards and takes with it some of the melt, which crystallizes as a single rod-like crystal, from which the stones are cut. The rare-earth garnets, lithium niobate and scheelite are grown by this method. A variation of the melt technique, little used for gem crystals, is carried out by gradually lowering a crucible of molten rare material to a cooler zone of the furnace where it crystallizes.

The most common method used to grow crystals from a solution is the hydro-thermal method, which depends upon the fact that water will attain much higher temperatures under pressure than it can at atmospheric pressure. This super-heated water will take mineral substances into solution which it would not under normal conditions. When the temperature is lowered, this super-saturated solution gives up some of the mineral, which then crystallizes on suitably placed seed crystals. An autoclave, a thick-walled "pressure bomb" which can be hermetically sealed, is used for this process, by which quartz and some emeralds are grown.

In the so-called flux-fusion method, the solvent consists of chemicals in which further chemicals necessary to produce the stone required are dissolved. Then the whole mixture is heated to a high temperature in a crucible. On cooling, the gem crystals crystallize out. This method produces well-formed crystals and is used to grow ruby, spinel, emerald and some rare-earth garnets, besides other less important stones.

The layman may well be awed by the number and types of synthetic stones on the market, and particularly by the multiplicity of trade names given them. The table on page 97 of the more important synthetic gemstones encountered in jewelers' shops may be of some help to readers.

Glass

The imitation of gemstones dates from the time of the Egyptians who used a glazed siliceous ware called faïence for such purposes. Today the material most commonly used for imitation gemstones is glass. Many types of glass are used. The cheapest type of imitation gems are made from crown-glass, like that used for windows. These glass stones, for which colorless glass may be used, are molded to shape. Some or all of their facets are then lightly polished, or they can be used straight from the mold. Some are mirrored on the back. As the mirror has a gold backing, the back of the stone appears gold. These mirrors are called *chatons* and are used to give a stone greater brilliancy, as this type of glass has little fire. Cheap glass imitation stones will reveal gas bubbles or swirls due to bad mixing of the glass when viewed with a lens.

The second type of glass used is flint glass, into which some lead oxide has been introduced. This gives a stone with considerable fire, but it is even softer than the cheap crown-glass stones. Furthermore, the lead content tends to darken by reaction with sulfide fumes from the atmosphere. Nowadays all glass imitation stones are referred to as paste, probably from presumably the Italian *pasta*, meaning dough, because nearly all glass stones are molded. The facet edges of molded stones appear rolled or rounded and to overcome this, some of them are polished on the

table facet or all of the crown facets. These are called tin-cut stones, presumably because they are polished on tin laps. A few glass stones have been fully cut from an unmolded lump of glass. These lapidary-cut stones are very beautiful.

Plastics

Plastics, including the so-called organic glasses, have been molded into faceted stones, mainly for costume jewelry but also for adorning costumes themselves. Apart from their softness—they are easily cut with a knife blade—they are very light in weight. This alone indicates that they are not genuine. But some plastics make excellent imitations of some ornamental gems. Bakelite, definitely the finest simulant of amber, is exceptional in that the plastic is heavier than the amber. Celluloid makes the finest imitation ivory.

Composite Stones

Let us end this chapter with a look at stones that are made of two or more parts. Such composite stones may be formed of two pieces and are known as doublets, or of three pieces, called triplets. Both types are made to imitate many different gems. Composite stones can be divided into several further categories. When stones are made of two pieces of similar material, such as two pieces of sapphire, they are called true doublets. Except for opal doublets, in which a thin layer of colorful opal is cemented to a base of common opal, true doublets are rare.

False doublets are made with a piece of real stone as the crown of the stone, cemented to a base of some inferior material. The diamond doublet is an example of a false doublet. The garnet-topped doublet is a variation of the false doublet in which a slice of red garnet is fused to a base of glass. The color of the glass determines the color of the stone. They are made in all colors.

STONE	GROWTH PROCESS	REMARKS
Diamond	High-pressure and high temperature	Not yet commercially produced in gem quality
Emerald	Flux-melt and hydrothermal	Characteristic feathers
Ruby	Verneuil flame-fusion, flux-fusion, and hydrothermal	Verneuil product detected by curved structure lines and gas bubbles; other methods by typical feathery inclusions
Sapphire	Verneuil flame-fusion	Curved bands and gas bubbles
Spinel	Verneuil flame-fusion and by flux-fusion	Colors not those of natural spinel. Red by Verneuil method shows curved bands. Flux-method has typical feathers
Quartz	Hydrothermal	Made colorless, blue, green and possibly brown-yellow
Rutile (Titania)	Verneuil flame-fusion	Made in all colors except green and violet, but colorless stones are always tinged yellow. Large doubling of the back facets and extreme fire
Strontium titanate (Fabulite and Diagem)	Verneuil flame-fusion	Rather soft and shows too much fire
Yttrium aluminate (YAG, Cirolite and Diamonair)	Pulled crystals from melt	Less fire than shown by diamond. Made colorless and in some colors
Lithium niobate (Linobate)	Pulled crystals from melt	Large doubling of the back facets and much fire. Colorless and other colors
Gadolinium gallium garnet (G.G.G., Galliant)	Pulled crystals from melt	Peach-colored under ultra-violet light

The doublets made to imitate ruby and sapphire are constructed with a crown of natural greenish-yellow sapphire with either a base of synthetic ruby or synthetic blue sapphire and are a recent development.

The so-called soudé stones, of which there are again three types, are more important. The first kind is made with a crown and pavilion of rock crystal with a colored layer, usually green, between them, along the girdle. In the second type the rock crystal is replaced by two pieces of synthetic colorless spinel. When these stones first came on the market in 1951, they were called in French *soudé sur spinelle* (soldered on spinel). More recently the synthetic spinel has been replaced by two pieces of pale emerald or pale aquamarine. These composite stones are usually made in green to imitate emerald, but those of synthetic spinel have been made in several different colors, even black.

Doublets can be detected quite easily or be remarkably difficult to identify, particularly if set. Soudé-type stones, called triplets in some countries, clearly show the colorless parts with a dark line of color between, if immersed in water and viewed sideways. This is not so simple when the stone is in a setting. Garnet-topped doublets are often made with the garnet top asymmetrically placed, so that when the side top facets are examined with a lens the join between garnet and glass is visible and the garnet shows a much higher luster than the glass.

Two unusual kinds of triplet must be mentioned. The first is made of white translucent jadeite and consists of a kernel capped by a hollow cabochon and finished with a base piece. The components are joined together with green-colored cement. The joins are readily visible when it is unset and adequate proof of the nature of the stone, but when in a setting they are most difficult to see. The second kind of stone consists of a cabochon of pale star rose quartz to the back of which is cemented a blue-colored base with a reflecting surface. This is the star rose quartz doublet, made to simulate a star sapphire. It is easy to distinguish, for when illuminated by a single overhead lamp bulb, an image of the bulb is seen at the crossing of the six-rayed star. You do not get this effect with a natural star sapphire.

18. Pearl

PEARL IS nearly as important as diamond, but many of its characteristics distinguish it from the other gem materials we have already discussed. Its origin is different, since it is the product of a living creature and has a beauty not found in other gems. What is more, this beauty does not need a lapidary's skill to bring it out. It is common knowledge that pearls come from oysters, though this is only partly true, for many different kinds of pearl are used in jewelry and not all come from oysters. To a biologist a pearl is any concretion, pearly or otherwise, found in mollusks. This accounts for the reports of pearls being found in edible oysters and mussels. But such objects have no place in the world of ornamentation, unless they have a pearly luster or attractive color.

The biological process by which a pearl is formed is set going by the animal's desire to overcome the intrusion of a foreign body. The popular idea that this is a grain of sand or a broken piece of shell is not strictly true. Scientific investigation has shown that it is generally started by a minute creature, a microscopic larval worm found in seas, rivers and lakes. To understand the process of pearl formation fully it is necessary to know something about the animal's structure.

The oyster is a soft-bodied creature with no rigid bony structure. It has two large muscles attached to the shell, which enable it to pull the two halves of the shell together and close them. It also has a foot, which by muscular contraction and expansion allows it to move slowly over the rocky bed. Near the foot is a gland which secretes a bunch of fibers, the *byssus*, which enables the oyster to attach itself to rocks. The most important part of the oyster is the mantle, a double flap of cellular tissue which envelops it inside the shell. This mantle is instrumental in forming pearls, though its true function is to secrete the materials which form the shell. Mollusks can be univalve, with a single shell, like a sea snail, or bivalve, when there are two shells joined by a hinge, as in the oyster and mussel.

The shell normally has three distinct layers. The outer horny layer is called the *periostracum*. The central layer is composed of prismatic crystals of calcium carbonate, usually in the form of calcite, identical in composition and crystalline structure to marble. This is known as the prismatic layer. Like the outer layer it does not increase in thickness once it is formed. The inner highly polished and sometimes brilliantly iridescent layers, which increase in thickness with the animal's age, are known as nacre, the so-called mother-of-pearl. These layers consist of another type of calcium carbonate called aragonite. The materials from which the shells are formed are obtained from the tissues of the minute organisms called plankton, upon which the animal feeds.

These materials are said to be separated from the animal's blood as it circulates through the mantle, which can excrete them in their fluid state upon its outer surface, where they subsequently solidify and harden into shell. Though this is the most generally accepted theory, an-

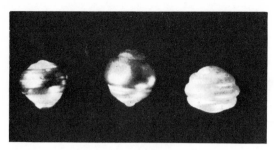

Round-a-Circle Pearls

Baroque Pearls

Twin Pearls

Button Pearls

Half (Blister) Pearls

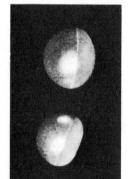

Three-Quarter Pearls

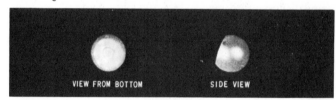

VIEW FROM BOTTOM   SIDE VIEW

Round Pearls   Drop Pearls   Pear-shaped

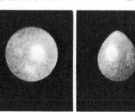

Different shapes of pearls.

other idea suggests that the fluid is secreted in the outer cells and interstices of the mantle, which afterwards separates. The organic matter which forms the outer horny layer of the shell is made of a substance called conchiolin, very similar to that forming hair and finger nails. It has been found that the tiny crystallites of aragonite which form the larger part of the shell are bonded together with a cement of conchiolin. This makes the second theory more tenable.

Some idea of the biological function of the mantle and the structure of the shell is essential for a fuller understanding of the formation of pearls. If an inanimate object or a small sea animal penetrates between the oyster's mantle and its shell, it irritates the animal. To alleviate this irritation, the oyster secretes a flow of fluid from the mantle, which hardens into nacre. This covers the intrusion and forms a smooth surface less irritating to the oyster's soft body, though it forms a bump on the shell. Such an excrescence on the shell, which can be very irregular in shape or almost round and dome-shaped, produces a blister pearl when removed from the shell, usually backed by a piece of mother-of-pearl. These blisters are mounted in jewelry, often with a closed-back setting to hide the unsightly back.

If the cause of the irritation is a minute larval worm, the oyster's endeavors to cement the intruder to the shell are less successful. It therefore reacts in another way, encysting the intruder in its body. In so doing it produces a fully nacreous pearl, sometimes known as a cyst pearl. A cyst pearl forms in stages. First a depression is formed in the mantle in which the wriggler gets trapped. Then the depression containing the worm deepens to form a bag. Finally, the neck of the bag joins up and forms a cyst in the animal's body. The perforation in the surface of the mantle heals over.

As you will realize, this cyst is lined with mantle tissue, which is inverted so that the secret-ing cell surface is inside and can secrete nacre over the entombed worm. Layer after layer of this secretion produces a pearl. This pearl sac, as the cyst is called, is essential for the formation of a cyst or whole pearl.

The oyster which produces the prized Oriental pearls is found in the waters of the Persian Gulf and the Gulf of Manaar, which separates Ceylon from India. It is the small oyster called *Pinctada radiata*. As its shell is only about 3 in. (7.5 cm.) across, it is obvious that it can never produce large pearls. Pearls about $1\frac{5}{8}$ inches (7 mm.) in diameter are about the largest. *Pinctada margaritifera* has a much larger shell, up to 8 in. (20 cm.) across and can produce relatively large pearls. This oyster is more widely distributed in tropical waters. The largest pearl oyster is *Pinctada maxima* which is found along the northern coast of Australia, the Torres Strait and out towards the Pacific islands of Micronesia. These oysters often have shells 12 to 14 in. (30 to 35 cm.) across and produce large pearls, which are much whiter than the delicately tinted Oriental pearls.

Other marine mollusks produce pearls, which are occasionally used in jewelry. The most important of these is the queen conch, *Strombus gigas*, a large snail-like univalve whose shell has a pink non-nacreous china-textured inner surface. It abounds in the waters around Florida and the West Indies and produces the non-nacreous pink conch pearls used in jewelry. Another animal, which provides highly colored green, blue and sometimes yellow nacreous pearls is *Haliotis*, commonly known as the ear shell. This animal is a univalve with a low-domed oval shell with a line of holes along one edge. The Channel Islands ormer is one type of this animal, though the larger specimens from tropical waters provide the colorful shells. Colorful pearls from Haliotis are occasionally strung into necklaces or mounted as pendants, but they usually have the disadvantage of being hollow.

(Left) "Mabe" pearls are pearls which are attached to the shell of the oyster instead of lying within the oyster's flesh. Mabe pearls are often called blister or half pearls because they are flat on one side. The pearl is sawn out of the shell and used in mountings which conceal the flat back of the pearl. Here, four mabe pearls are used in an opulent necklace. (Right) Black pearls are extremely scarce. Very few are found each year. Scientists have discovered that black pearls can be formed by irradiating pearl oysters with X-rays; however, these often lack luster. Most black pearls on the market today are dyed, and must be identified as such.

Freshwater pearls are obtained from a number of freshwater shell-bearing mollusks which abound in rivers and lakes all over the world. From the mussel *Unio* come the freshwater pearls of Scotland, Ireland and Wales. Pearls from freshwater shellfish have not the same beauty as deep-sea pearls, but when of good quality have their own attractiveness. One interesting group of them are the pearls found in certain shellfish that live in the tributaries of the Mississippi River. Many of them have a fine luster and color and are often found in bizarre shapes like bird's wings and dog's teeth, eminently suitable for making floral designs in jewelry.

The picturesque and primitive way of fishing for pearls in the Persian Gulf and in the waters off India and Ceylon has rapidly declined, now that safer and more profitable employment is available there. The sight of a man diving from a boat, protected only by a nose clip, with a stone weight to carry him down to the bottom and a bag to collect the oysters, is practically a thing of the past. The stench of oyster flesh rotting before it is washed away and the residue searched by hand for pearls are now rarely encountered. The Western market no longer sees the lovely Bombay bunches of drilled pearls, which used to come to the pearl dealers in Paris and London.

The Australian and Pacific pearl fisheries have been more fortunate. In these waters, the thick shells as well as the pearls produce revenue. They supply the mother-of-pearl so widely used for buttons and ornamentation. True, the demand

Freshwater pearl clams produce tiny, delicate pearls. This mollusk spent most of its life suspended in a plastic basket in the fresh waters of Lake Biwa, Japan, where most freshwater pearls are produced (hence the name "Biwako" pearls).

for pearl buttons has declined with the coming of plastics and this has not helped the Australian trade.

Sailing luggers with auxiliary engines are used in the Australian, Torres Strait and Pacific fisheries and the divers use armored diving suits. The oysters brought from the sea bed are opened and searched for pearls, which are sold to a pearl buyer when the lugger returns to port. Any pearls with commercially acceptable blisters, known as chicot pearls, are kept separate for the blister to be removed. Most blisters are hollow and known as mud blisters, but some are solid, and on rare occasions removal of their outer skins has revealed valuable pearls inside.

Pearls can vary considerably in shape. Round pearls are used for necklaces, while pear- or drop-shaped pearls are more suitable for pendants and earrings. Button or bouton pearls, which have one side somewhat flattened, are used for rings, studs, ear studs and the center pearls of brooches. Pearls of irregular shape are termed baroque or barrok pearls. Small pearls that weigh less than $\frac{1}{4}$ grain are termed seed pearls. Natural pearls are weighed in pearl grains, each $\frac{1}{4}$ carat.

To explain many of the effects which give pearls their incomparable beauty and to understand what conditions can harm them, one needs to know something of their nature and structure. Pearls are soft and easily damaged, though they will withstand ordinary wear if given normal care. The major constituent of pearls is calcium carbonate, which is very susceptible to acids, so an acid skin or excessive use of certain kinds of cosmetics can break down their surface. This erosion is shown by the barrel shape of the pearls near the clasp in pearl necklaces, as they are the ones that lie close to the skin of the neck and are more likely to be eroded away.

If a pearl is rubbed across one's teeth, its surface feels gritty. This is because the nacre of pearls is built up of overlapping platelets of aragonite. The irregular edges seem like a fine file to sensitive teeth. This test will tell whether a pearl is real or an imitation, for an imitation pearl feels smooth when tested like this. But this test cannot differentiate between real and cultured pearls, for both have a nacreous skin.

The porcelain-like pink conch pearls do not grit on the teeth either, but are easily identified by the flame-like markings on their surfaces,

103

which also distinguish them from coral, which has straight banding and no flame-markings. These serrated edges of the overlapping platelets on the surface of nacreous pearls diffract the light and produce the optical effect called the *orient* of pearls. A pearl with a good orient is called a ripe pearl, one with an imperfect display, an unripe pearl.

Pearls are usually white, particularly Australian pearls, but pearls from the Persian Gulf and the waters around Ceylon are often tinged with an imperceptible pinkish hue, termed rosée. These pearls are highly prized. Some pearls are tinged with yellow and more appreciated by darker-skinned women. Pearls with a pronounced coloring such as pinks, blues, yellow and black are rarer. The latter, sometimes an attractive bronze shade, come from the waters of the Gulf of California, though they are sometimes found elsewhere. The cause of the color of these pearls is largely unknown. There are many theories but little proof.

A dark slaty-blue pearl is termed a blue pearl. Its color is caused by a layer of dark conchiolin just beneath its translucent surface layers or by a conchiolin-rich center. A pearl with a center containing mud or silt may also produce a blue pearl, sometimes called a mud or silt pearl. Pearls can be artificially colored rosée by the careful use of eosin dyes, or black with silver nitrate, which is reduced to black silver by the action of the conchiolin and light.

Let me close this chapter with a few hints on the care of pearls:

1. Keep pearls loosely wrapped in non-acid tissue paper. Never let them rub against other jewelry in a jewel case.
2. After a pearl necklace has been worn, rub it lightly with a clean chamois skin to remove dust and perspiration before it is put away.
3. Necklaces should be cleaned and restrung by a professional pearl stringer at least once a year.
4. Do not shut up pearls in a case or strong box for years. Light and air are essential for the preservation of their luster.
5. Never subject pearls to heat. It is surprising how little is needed to burn a pearl and turn it brown and useless.

The intriguing shapes of large baroque pearls present a challenge to the jewelry designer. Here they are imaginatively used in an elegant pearl bracelet.

19. The Cultured Pearl

THE DAY OF THE NATURAL PEARL is not over, but it has certainly waned. For economic and social reasons the cultured pearl is the pearl of the century. The first cultured pearls appeared as early as the 13th century, when the Chinese found that by forcing open the valves (shells) of a freshwater mussel, *Cristaria plicata*, and inserting an object between the shell and the mantle, the animal, on being returned to the water for some months, would cover it with nacre and cement it to the shell. Much later a trade was carried on in small metal images of Buddha treated like this. They were sold as amulets or tourist pieces.

During the last decade of the 19th century, the Japanese continued the old Chinese method, using their small oyster, *Pinctada martensi*. They cemented small mother-of-pearl beads onto the shell, which after the animal had been returned to the water for a few years were found to be coated with nacre. The beads were then cut from the shell and the non-nacreous back part ground flat and sometimes drilled in the center to take a plug. The back was finished with a piece of mother-of-pearl ground to symmetrical shape. Such pearls, then known as Japanese pearls but nowadays more correctly as cultured blistered pearls, can be deceptive when mounted in a close back setting. This was the start of the Japanese cultured pearl industry.

The type of cultured blister pearl commonly marketed today is the mabe pearl, which was actually produced as early as 1902. Modern mabe pearls are grown on the shell of the large Australian oyster, *Pinctada maxima*. A half sphere of soft steatite is cemented onto the shell and the animal is then returned to the sea for some time. When it is fished up again, the bead is found to be coated with nacre. This blister is then removed by sawing round it with a trepan saw. The nucleus is removed and the internal surface of the nacre shell is cleaned of all extraneous matter. If necessary, the inside of the nacreous shell is tinted.

A smaller round mother-of-pearl bead is then cemented inside in place of the original bead with a white cement. The inset gives the pearl solidity. The base is then completed with a ground and polished hemispherical piece of mother-of-pearl. Of the several advantages of producing blister pearls in this way, the most important is that the dark conchiolin is cleaned from inside the nacre shell, giving a much whiter pearl.

The aim of many scientific workers in Japan and many other parts of the world, was to produce a fully spherical cultured pearl. In Japan a team of scientists, inspired by Kokichi Mikimoto, eventually produced a cultured cyst pearl. Such pearls are said to have been commercially produced in 1913, but none reached the West until about 1921. This presented a problem of detection, for the completed cultured pearl consists of a large core of mother-of-pearl completely covered with nacre. Outwardly it shows little sign of the core within.

As explained earlier, a pearl-sac is essential to obtain a cyst or spherical pearl, so in cultivating such pearls an artificial pearl-sac must be made.

The earliest way of producing one was the so-called all-lapped method. This entailed making an artificial sac by cutting the mantle away from one oyster, which killed it, then cutting up the mantle into pieces of suitable size to form a bag to take a mother-of-pearl bead. The bag containing the bead was then inserted in another oyster through an incision made in its body. This oyster was returned to the sea for some three years, then retrieved and the cultured pearl removed.

This method was found to waste too many oysters. The more recent piece method is now always used. Instead of using a large piece of mantle to envelop the bead, the mantle of one

(Left) Pegs being inserted in oysters which have been suspended in baskets beneath rafts floating in Ago Bay, near Osaka, Honshu, Japan, so that they will remain open for the delicate nucleus operation shown below, the start of the cultured pearl. (Below) The pig-toe squares are polished in four stages until they become smooth spheres. Prepared in various sizes, the gleaming white nuclei are then ready for the pearl farmers.

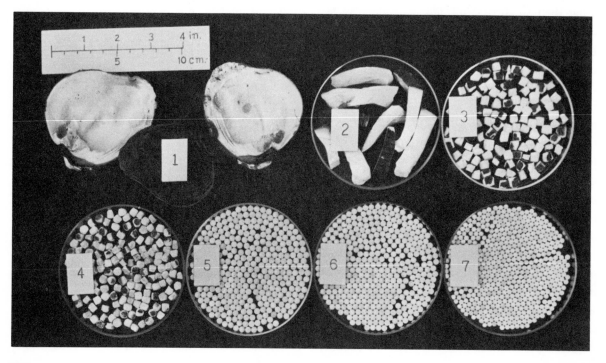

That part of the mantle which secretes nacre is cut from a live oyster. With the rough edges trimmed away, the tissue is cut into 15 to 20 tiny squares. Each square will be inserted together with a nucleus in another oyster. (Sometimes two squares and two nuclei are used.) The "foreign" tissue will form a "pearl sac" about the nucleus until a pearl has been formed.

oyster is removed and cut into tiny squares. One of these squares is inserted in the animal's body and a bead is pressed on top of it to form the nucleus. The square of mantle quickly grows round the mother-of-pearl bead to form the pearl-sac. Cultivation is then the same as for the all-lapped process.

Good quality cultured pearls can only be obtained from healthy oysters. To keep them healthy and guard them from other sea creatures, the oysters are kept in cages in "farms." Ago Bay on the southern coast of Honshu is the center of the Japanese cultured pearl industry. The small oyster, *Pinctada martensi*, is cultivated. But Japan is now not the only place where pearls are cultivated. Experiments were also carried out outside Japanese territorial waters. They used the larger oysters, *Pinctada margaritifera* and *Pinctada maxima*, to produce large cultured pearls in the waters around the Palau Islands in the Pacific Ocean between World Wars I and II.

In 1956 a cultured pearl farm was started in Kuri Bay, near Brecknock Harbour in north-western Australia, using the large *Pinctada maxima*. These larger animals seem to deposit the nacre more quickly. A suitable thickness of coating is produced in two years (rather than the small Japanese oyster's three) and much larger pearls are produced. Since the similar cultured pearl farms have been established in the Mergui Archipelago off southern Burma, the Palau farms have been restarted.

Pearls without a bead nucleus have been successfully cultivated, too. This project was started by the Japanese in the freshwater lake of Biwa, using the freshwater mussel, *Hyropsis schegeli*. These pearls are propagated by inserting a small piece of mantle tissue into the edge of the animal's mantle. This sets up sufficient irritation to start the animal secreting nacre around it. The pearls produced are usually orange when first removed from the mussel, but this color fades, quickly or slowly, and then they may be treated to bring them to an agreeable light rosy cream color. They do not seem to be dyed.

These non-nucleated cultured pearls are generally small and usually bun-shaped or baroque and quite bright, with a pleasing orient. They are nearly always drilled and strung into necklaces, or on wires to form brooches, pendants and other articles. Most are sold in Arab countries and marketed mainly through Beirut, Lebanon. Successful attempts have been made to produce non-nucleated cultured pearls in Australian waters using large oysters, but though the pearls are large and whiter and baroque or oval in shape, production seems small.

A Mikimoto technician inserts an artificial nucleus—a bead made of the shell of the Mississippi River mussel—into the body of an oyster. The oyster will be replaced in a basket hanging under a raft and will cover the bead with pearl nacre.

Their general appearance may help in identifying cultured pearls, but many of them are not obvious. Though poor quality cultured pearls are fairly easy to detect by their appearance, those of better quality may need the services of the technical staff of a fully equipped laboratory to prove whether they are natural or cultured. Many of the medium and low-quality cultured pearls have a significantly greenish or yellowish tinge. This not very pleasing color is probably due to the layer of conchiolin which the animal usually secretes over the bead nucleus and is visible through the overlying translucent layers of nacre.

It might be thought that the thicker the deposit of nacre, the better the pearl's color, but this is not always so. The color is really controlled by the thickness of the conchiolin layer round the bead nucleus. If it is thick and dark-colored, the pearl appears dark, if thin and light, a good quality pearl results. The thickness of the translucent nacreous layer is less important, provided it is thick enough to withstand normal wear.

The surface of cultured pearls often shows subcutaneous markings reminiscent of varicose veins. Piqué marks—small dimples often seen on genuine pearls and assumed to be a sign of their genuineness—should not be relied upon, as they have been seen on cultured pearls. If a cultured pearl necklace is held out horizontally under a strong light, perhaps a desk lamp, and the beads are rotated, some of the pearls will show the telltale sheen of the mother-of-pearl beads if the skins are not too thick, proving the pearls are cultured. Accurate identification of pearls needs elaborate X-ray and optical apparatus operated by experienced technologists.

Cultured pearls can be treated to make them whiter. This is usually done by drilling obliquely through the pearl towards the discontinuation layer between the bead and the nacreous outer layer and injecting a chemical that keeps down the color of the conchiolin. Pearls can be tinted, too, usually a rosée shade, or black, the latter with silver nitrate or, as recently reported, by emanations from the radio-isotope cobalt 60.

Cultured pearls should be cared for in the same way as natural pearls. But barrel-shaped wear is more serious in cultured pearls as it eventually leaves the bead nucleus exposed around the periphery of the pearl. The cups of nacre left at each side will readily part from the core. Another danger is that heavy grease from cosmetics can travel through the string canal along the discontinuation layer of conchiolin around the bead nucleus. The grease readily collects dirt, so it becomes dark and may show through the translucent overlying nacre. The pearls then

After about 3½ years, the pearl will have covered the bead nucleus with an acceptable layer of pearl nacre. It is then removed from the water and the cultured pearl removed. It will be inspected and graded for color and size before going to the jeweler. The oyster itself is discarded.

look dark and unattractive. They can be cleaned but this takes time and skill. Anyway, cultured pearl necklaces like those of natural pearl should be periodically cleaned and restrung.

To conclude this chapter something must be said of the various kinds of imitation pearl. The earlier type is the hollow-glass bead which seems to have been discontinued about 1930, although they may still be met in old jewelry. They were constructed of a hollow sphere of glass, coated inside with pearl essence, a suspension of guanine crystals obtained from fish scales in parchment size. The rest of the hollow shell was filled with wax. These hollow-glass imitation pearls were quite effective but easily broken. They were easy to detect, as a lens revealed the broken edges of the glass at the string hole, as well as bubbles in the glass sphere. Lastly, a spot of ink placed on the surface would appear double, as it was reflected at the lower surface of the thin glass sphere.

The modern imitation pearl consists of a solid glass bead over which a layer of pearl essence—either the old fish scale essence or the newly-developed synthetic pearl essence—bonded in cellulose lacquer is sprayed, or coated by dipping. Attempts have been made to use plastic beads as cores, but the very light weight of plastic does not allow necklaces of them to hang well on the neck. Mother-of-pearl beads, as used for the nucleus of cultured pearls, are more successful. Necklaces of these shell-based imitation pearls have been sold as imitation cultured pearls.

All these externally coated imitation pearls are easily detected by the blotting paper appearance of the surface when viewed with a lens. Examination of the coating near the string hole will show it has worn away where it has been rubbed by the next pearl. Imitation pearls of both the earlier and more modern types feel smooth when rubbed over the teeth, though one make of these pearls is said to grit on the teeth to some extent.

Small pieces of mother-of-pearl cut from certain sea shells are also used for pearls in cheap jewelry. These Antilles pearls, as they are called,

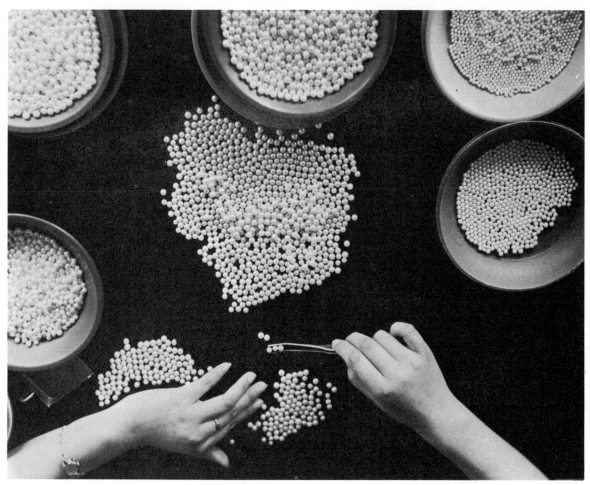

After the pearls are sorted for quality and hue, they are divided according to size and shape. A special tool helps the sorter.

are pearly at the top but non-nacreous underneath. Another object, rarely encountered, is the coque-de-perle, which consists of part of the whorl of a nautilus shell which looks like a form of blister pearl when filled with cement to make it solid. You would not imagine that a metal ore could imitate a pearl, but polished spheres of the iron mineral called hematite have been used to imitate black pearls. They can be distinguished by their heavier weight, but even more conclusively by the red streak they leave when rubbed on a piece of unglazed white porcelain.

20. Other Gems from Living Things

THE MOST IMPORTANT GEM of organic origin is undoubtedly the pearl. It is so well known in the world of jewelry that it demanded the two previous chapters to itself. There are other organic gem materials, although of lesser importance and value, that are encountered every so often.

Amber

The first of these is amber, a fossil resin from ancient pine trees. It is known from artifacts found in ancient tombs that its history goes back to centuries before the birth of Christ and that its use was worldwide. As it is a soft material, it can be easily worked and carved. Amber varies in color from white through pale yellow to reddish and yellowish brown. Black and green colors are also known and one variety, called osseous amber, has the appearance of bone. Amber varies from a clear, nearly transparent, material to one that is translucent and at its worst, cloudy.

The majority of amber comes from the Samland coast of the eastern Baltic in the vicinity of the town of Kaliningrad, Russia, where it is mined from a green sandy rock called glauconite. It is also washed out by wave action from the local sea bed. Such pieces are picked up on the shore. Amber is only slightly heavier than water with the result that tides and currents take it along the shores of the Baltic as far as the North Sea. This accounts for the finding of amber along the eastern seaboard of England. Another source of amber is the neighborhood of Catania in Sicily, where it is called simetite. A type called burmite is found in northern Burma. Other deposits known have no trade significance.

Clear amber is rare in large pieces. Cloudy amber, which owes its cloudiness to many gas bubbles, may be clarified by heating it in rape seed oil. This is done commercially. If the treatment is not carefully done, stress cracks, called sun spangles may be produced. These cracks resemble the leaves of the nasturtium. Clear pieces of amber with sun spangles can be very pretty and are sometimes cut and polished. If dyes are introduced to color the "leaves" red or green, the treated amber is sometimes called Chinese amber, but it has no connection with China.

When amber is heated to about 180°C. (356°F.) it becomes tacky, so small unusable pieces of amber are consolidated by heating them in a hydraulic press to produce much larger pieces. The result is pressed amber.

As amber started life as a resin oozing out of pine trees it often collected pine needles, vegetable debris and insects. Even the mineral pyrites in the form of small crystals has been found entombed. The fly in the amber is proverbial but good specimens are rare. Furthermore, because an amber-like material contains an insect, this is no proof that the piece is amber. Copal resin, a natural resin of recent origin, which is sometimes used to simulate the true amber, often has insects included in it. Even a scorpion has been found entombed in a piece of kauri gum, which is a copal resin from the kauri pine of New Zealand. In recent years, some of the glass-like plastics have been formed around insects, often of large size, and mounted in jewelry. However, they tend to show a crazed surface after some time.

Amber is also commonly imitated by man-made plastics, the most common and deceptive being a suitably colored clear bakelite. From this material, which has a typical red to reddish-brown color, many of the "amber" necklaces on sale are made. Celluloid, as well as some of the "organic glasses," and the milk plastic casein, when clear and suitably colored, have been used to simulate amber.

Applying a knife blade to an inconspicuous part of the specimen, such as the drill hole in the case of beads, can tell a lot. Amber comes away in small chips or powder, and so does copal resin. Bakelite peels or chips into larger pieces and is somewhat tough to the knife, while most of the other plastic imitations tend to peel easily. Copal resin tends after a time to craze all over the surface as do many of the glass-like plastics; moreover, when the surface of copal resin is briskly rubbed it tends to become sticky. Similar treatment with celluloid tends to give off a smell of camphor. An amber-colored glass is too hard to be touched with a knife blade so may be readily distinguished. The oft-repeated belief that when amber is rubbed it will electrify and pick up bits of paper, while true, is not a test for amber because most of the simulants will behave similarly.

Jet

The intense black fossil vegetable product called jet is allied to brown coal. Jet is soft, yet takes an exceptionally good polish so that it is little wonder that from ancient times it was a favorite among local craftsmen. It is found mainly in the shales along the Yorkshire coast near Whitby, England. Another important source is the province of Asturias in Spain, and small quantities are found in France, Germany and other places throughout the eastern and western hemispheres.

As far as England is concerned, jet had its heyday during the latter half of the reign of Queen Victoria, although it was known much earlier. The Romans are believed to have taken jet from Whitby when they occupied England. They knew the material because they had made decorative articles earlier from the jet they found in Asia Minor.

A good test for jet is to apply a hot needle to an inconspicuous part of the object. The odor of burning coal will supply the answer. Vulcanite, the hard black type of rubber used as an imitation of jet, when heated the same way will give off a strong smell of burning rubber. Bakelite, if affected at all, will smell of carbolic. Black onyx and black glass, other simulants, are far too hard; they will resist a knife blade, while jet will chip.

Coral

Although coral is well known in a variety of natural forms and colors, few of them are suitable for the jeweler's art. Coral has been described as the skeletons of small sea creatures. Actually, it is the calcareous structure built up by secretions from anemone-like marine organisms called polyps. These structures, often like trees, are truly the homes of the polyps. The variety known as *Corallium rubrum*, or *Corallium nobili*, produces the white to red coral used in jewelry. Coral polyps grow in warm waters and the fisheries are mainly in the western Mediterranean between Italy and the North African coast. Today much coral used for jewelry and small carvings comes from the

Gold jewelry set with diamonds and also (top right) with unusual gem materials for rings, ivory and ebony. Designers, from the top, were Graham Harron, Paul Raun, and Alison Richards.

waters around Japan and Malaysia. The Mediterranean fisheries are an Italian industry which operates from Torre del Greco just south of Naples, and it is here that most of the coral is fashioned, and even Japanese coral is imported to Italy for fashioning, although more and more red coral is being carved in the Orient.

Rose-pink hues, especially, are the most prized colors of coral, especially the delicate pale pink known as angel's skin. The deep red coral is much used for small carvings, although in some parts of the world pure white is preferred. Much white coral, especially that found in Japanese waters, is artificially stained to a red or pink shade, which is said to fade in time. Small pieces of thin branches of red coral which are polished, drilled across the center of the branch and strung into necklaces, are called Arabian beads. A black coral is fished from many waters, particularly those around Hawaii and this coral, which is horny and not calcareous like precious coral, has been fashioned for jewelry.

The difference between pink conch pearl and coral has already been described. It is the only other natural product which can imitate coral, except perhaps for a piece of sea shell suitably cut and shaped or a suitably stained ivory. Other imitations of coral are legion. They are anything from sealing wax to dyed gypsum, and various other compressed mixtures. Unexpected, but not uncommon, is an imitation made from stained vegetable ivory. This is easily identified by the dot-like cell structures, which are made more prominent by the dyestuff, when the beads —and they are mostly seen as bead necklaces—are examined with a hand lens. Coral, too, will fizz when a spot of acid is placed on it, as does the pink pearl, but the horny type of black coral does not react, neither do the coral fakes.

Tortoise-Shell

Despite its name, tortoise-shell does not come from a tortoise, but is obtained from the carapace of the hawk's-bill turtle which is found mainly in the islands of Indonesia, particularly Sulawesi, an island long known as Celebes. Nothing else compares with its beautiful mottling in yellows, reddish-browns, and browns. The shell from the plastron, the underbelly plate, is clear yellow and is known as blond shell.

Most simulants of tortoise-shell are plastics.

Plastic imitations are not hard to identify, because the color is made up of broad swaths. The color mottling of true tortoise-shell is made up of small brownish disks and the thicker they are massed together the deeper the brown color. These dots may be seen with a lens or may need a microscope to resolve them. The most difficult simulant to spot consists of a thin sheet of real tortoise-shell bonded to a thicker sheet of plastic. Dyed translucent horn is another.

Tortoise-shell will soften in boiling water. This treatment is used to decorate it by embedding inlays of mother-of-pearl or metal wires. A variation of this is the silver pins inserted in tortoise-shell and called piqué-work, seen in some older ornaments and 18th-century watch cases.

Sea Shells

The shells of the queen conch, the animal which produces pink conch pearls and the helmet shell, are two sea shells from which the ever popular shell cameos are cut. The first gives a white carving on a pink background, and the second is white on a brown background. The thick central columns of some sea shells are formed into beads and strung into necklaces. These may be quite attractive, and so are the small top-shells which have had their outside "skins" removed to reveal the iridescent mother-of-pearl. These are also strung into necklaces.

Shell cat's-eyes are of two types. The first is a dark purplish mother-of-pearl which, when cut as cabochons, show a vague ray of light across them. These are of little importance and of no value, but they sometimes are met as buttons. The second type, sometimes called Chinese cat's-eyes, are porcelain-like disks with a dome-shaped top. They are prettily marked with green and brown, but do not have the cat's-eye effect. Chinese cat's-eyes are opercula, the name for the doors which certain sea snails use to close the entrance to their shells. They are found along the shores of most Pacific islands and have been used to embellish jewelry.

Ivory

The last substance which needs to be mentioned is ivory. It is a pure white substance which yellows with age and is actually the dentine of teeth. The best ivory is obtained from elephants' tusks, which are highly specialized teeth and grow to an extraordinary length. Ivory is a soft material. Although compact, it is permeated throughout with very fine pores which are filled with a gelatinous substance. The gelatinous substance helps to give ivory an excellent polish. Most ivory is obtained from the tusks of the African elephant and from the smaller tusks of the Indian elephant. A slightly harder and finer grained ivory is obtained from the teeth of the hippopotamus. Coarser types come from two marine mammals—the walrus and the narwhal. Ivory from these last two animals is used for carving by the inhabitants of Arctic regions. Mammoths, which roamed the north of Europe and Asia, have been found perfectly refrigerated in the ice of these regions of permafrost. Parts of their tusks have been found still usable as ivory, although it is slightly more brittle than recent ivory from modern elephants.

Because of its unique properties, ivory has been used by artists and craftsmen all over the world, throughout the centuries. Much has been written on the beautiful ivory carvings contained in the world's collections. The very appearance and feel of ivory indicate what it is. Few simulants are able to reach this degree of perfection. A test for true ivory are the intersecting curvilinear bands rather like engine turning seen when a section has been cut across the width of the tusk. In all worked ivory, there is sure to be one aspect in this direction. This is specific for elephant ivory. Longitudinal sections show straight banding, but so do other materials.

Ivory Simulants

Few other materials are prone to such a diverse number of simulants. Bone is one that can be rather difficult to detect from some of the coarser ivories, which can be rather like bone. However, bone does not have the luster and polish of ivory and, further, the surface is usually marked with "pits" where the bone canals have

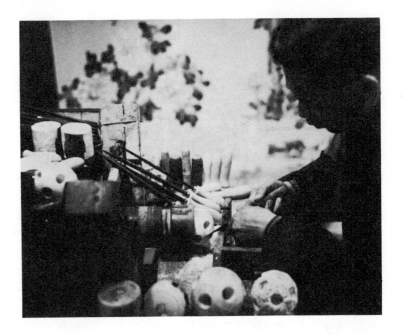

In Hong Kong, ivory balls are carved so that there are many loose intricately carved ones inside one another. It is done with a foot lathe and extremely sharp knives and hooks. This man carved a ball with 28 layers.

been cut across. Even coarser in structure is the "ivory" from the antler of the deer, so often used for carvings, especially in Germany and sometimes in Scotland.

An unusual ivory simulant is the material from the ivory-nut palm found growing in the tropical regions of South America. This so-called vegetable ivory is obtained from the nuts of the plant, which are the size of a turkey's egg. An ivory nut is similar to an oversized Brazil nut, with a brown outer skin and milk-white solid meat. It is too small to produce anything of size unless pieces of nuts are joined together for carving into small articles. The tell-tale dots of cellular growth give away its origin. Probably the most important of the ivory simulants is celluloid. It can be identified because it easily peels with a knife while ivory is tough. If a peeling of celluloid is held in a flame it will burn vigorously; ivory will not. Other types of plastics are employed to imitate ivory, but none so well as celluloid.

21. How Gems Are Tested

THE TESTING OF GEMSTONES is a complex matter needing some knowledge of a number of sciences. Only a few aspects of this vast subject can be explored here. There are several books devoted to the identification of gems. Probably the easiest method (although it is far from reliable) is to carry out a scratch test, as each mineral has its own degree of hardness. To do this, pointed fragments of minerals of known hardness, usually mounted in holders, are drawn across the stone in an unobtrusive place. The hardness of the stone will be between the mineral that will just scratch it and the next hardest, which will not. The scratch hardness scale of numbers, which was devised by the mineralogist Mohs, is as follows:

1.	Talc	6.	Feldspar
2.	Gypsum	7.	Quartz (Rock crystal)
3.	Calcite	8.	Topaz
4.	Fluorspar	9.	Sapphire
5.	Apatite	10.	Diamond

Window glass is about $5\frac{1}{2}$ and a steel file about $6\frac{1}{2}$.

A better method is to use polished plates of the scale mineral and find out the consecutive numbers that the stone will scratch and will not scratch. Hardness tests are difficult to carry out on faceted stones for the risk of damage is great, even if a test plate be used. The only real effective use of hardness testing is on such objects as carvings and other pieces which have a base or back where a scratch mark will not be noticeable. Some cases where hardness testing is useful have been mentioned earlier in this book.

When a stone is unset, the specific gravity, more commonly called the density, may be assessed. This is the ratio between the weight of a substance and the weight of an equal volume of water. A density determination is made by weighing the stone in the normal way in air, using an accurate balance, and making a second weighing with the stone suspended from the balance arm so that it dangles in a vessel of water. It will then be found to weigh less and the numerical difference between the two weighings divided into the weight of the stone in air will give the density. The densities of different stones are fairly constant and by reference to published tables the nature of the stone can be assessed. Simple as this appears to be, many precautions need to be taken. Also the test is not very accurate for small stones. Flotation methods using so-called heavy liquids are another method which is used, but these liquids are not easily obtainable. Moreover they are somewhat noxious.

The gemmologist—the name applied to the expert in gem testing—uses the behavior of light in a gemstone as a means of identifying it. This is mainly carried out by measuring the power that a stone has of bending a ray of light. Most readers will know that a stick partially immersed in water appears to bend at the surface of the air and water. This optical effect is due to the fact that a ray of light is bent when it enters or leaves a denser medium than air. Water is optically a little denser than air. The bending is called the refraction of light. The power of a substance to bend a ray of light is fairly constant, and in gemstones the bending is so constant that this provides a method of identification. A mathematical formula, known as Snell's Law, computes the bending power of a substance to a

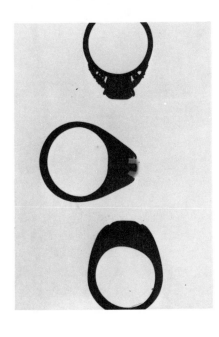

(Left) A positive method of testing a ring to see whether it is set with diamond or imitation diamond is to use X-rays because the diamond (center) is transparent to them, but not the imitations. (Right) Composite stones are made of two or three parts and provide one form of imitation stone. The one illustrated above is a "soudé emerald" and it consists of a top and base of rock crystal with a green layer between them. In liquid, the parts show up clearly.

ray of light. Optical instruments are made based on this formula to give a direct reading of the refractive index of the gem. One such instrument, the refractometer, is made specially for jewelers, but some knowledge of gem crystals is needed in order to get the best results from it.

What is probably the most modern method of gem testing is by the examination of the absorption spectrum using a small hand spectroscope. White light is made up of all the colored rays of the spectrum, which range through reds, yellows, oranges, greens, blues and violets. When a beam of white light enters, or is reflected from, a colored gemstone, the colors of the gem are transmitted to the eye and the remaining colors of the spectrum are absorbed by the stone.

A spectroscope analyses light. If white light is examined through it, all the colors of the spectrum, the rainbow colors, will be seen. But if this light has first passed through or has been reflected from a colored stone, certain colors, those absorbed by the stone, will be missing. The spectrum will therefore show vertical black bands or lines in the positions of the absorbed

colors. This is an absorption spectrum. Many gemstones show such a characteristic pattern in the absorption bands that they may be identified at once.

Also depending on the absorption bands of colored gemstones is a dichromatic filter called the Chelsea color filter. This small piece of equipment was discussed in the chapter about emeralds.

Without going even into simple crystallography, some of the more important methods used by the gemmologist cannot be properly explained. One that can be understood is double refraction. It occurs only in crystals, but not in all crystals. It is the phenomenon whereby a ray of light entering a stone splits into two rays which travel at slightly different angles within the stone. Thus anything looked at through such a stone will appear doubled. Zircon is doubly refracting and the rear facets looked at through the table will appear to be doubled.

Polarized light can be used to detect double refraction. Ordinary light vibrates in all directions at right angles to the direction of travel, while polarized light vibrates in one plane only.

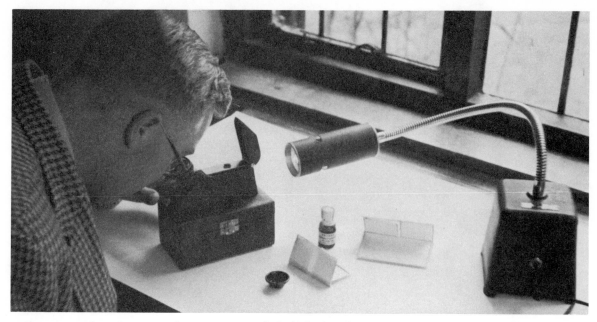

One way of testing gems is to measure their light-bending power with an instrument called a refractometer, which the better jewelers have in their shops. Not all gems can be checked with it.

Although there are special polarizing prisms for the job, a sheet of polaroid will produce adequate polarized light. For experiments with gemstones, the lenses from a pair of polaroid spectacles are sufficient. There are two ways of using polaroid to detect double refraction. The first is to examine the so-called dichroic effect. The two rays in a doubly refracting gemstone are not only plane polarized at right angles to each other, but in the case of colored stones, each ray may absorb light differently, either with different colors or with different shades of the same color. A stone is bathed in a strong white light and is viewed through a piece of polaroid. Rotating the polaroid causes it to select the vibration directions. As a result, the two colors will be seen one after another.

The second method uses two polaroid sheets, one above the other with a suitable distance between them for the insertion of the stone. The two polaroids must be arranged so that their vibration directions are at right angles to one another—the "crossed polars" position. It can

be readily found by turning the polaroid sheets until no or very little light comes through. When this is set up with a light source below the lower polaroid sheet, the stone is held between the two polars and rotated. Singly refractive stones will show dark all the time, but doubly refractive stones will show a very convincing four times light and four times dark during a complete revolution of the stone. Some singly refractive stones may show patchy areas of dark and light caused by strain in the material. This is confusing, but the effect is never so clear as with doubly refracting stones.

A number of other techniques are employed by the gemmologist, such as the characteristic luminescence (glow of light) emitted from some stones when they are bathed in a beam of ultraviolet light. Some chemical tests are occasionally used. X-rays are particularly important for the testing of pearls and sometimes for gemstones. These techniques are for the professional gemmologist only.

White Stones

	H.	S.G.	R.I.	Ref.	D.	Remarks
Alabaster	2	2.32	1.53	Double	Tl	An ornamental stone.
Bakelite	$2\frac{1}{2}$	1.28	1.65	Single	O	Carbolic smell when heated.
Casein	$2\frac{1}{2}$	1.33	1.55	Single	O	Smells of burnt milk when heated.
Celluloid	2	1.35	1.50	Single	Tl	Easily flames.
Chalcedony	7	2.62	1.53	Double	Tl	May imitate some moonstone.
Coral	$3\frac{1}{2}$	2.68	—	—	O	Effervesces with acid.
Ivory	$2\frac{1}{2}$	1.8	1.54	—	Tl	Typical curved markings.
Jadeite	7	3.34	1.65	Double	Tl	Surface shows dimpled structure.
Marble	3	2.71	1.50	Double	O	Effervesces with acid.
Meerschaum	2	1.5	1.53	—	O	Porous and floats on water.
Nephrite	$6\frac{1}{2}$	3.00	1.61	Double	Tl	Lower density than jadeite.
Pearl	$3\frac{1}{2}$	2.70	—	—	O	Shows irregular edges of platelets.
Quartz	7	2.65	1.55	Double	Tl	Sometimes contains gold.

LEGEND:—H.=Hardness; S.G.=Specific gravity; R.I.=Refractive indices; Ref.=Refraction; D.=Diaphaneity; V=Variable; T.=Transparent; Tl.=Translucent; O.=Opaque.

Brown Stones

	H.	S.G.	R.I.	Ref.	D.	Remarks
Amber	$2\frac{1}{2}$	1.08	1.54	Single	Tl	Imitated by bakelite.
Bakelite	$2\frac{1}{2}$	1.28	1.65	Single	Tl	Carbolic smell when heated.
Cairngorm	7	2.65	1.54–1.55	Double	T	Density and refractive indices identify.
Casein	$2\frac{1}{2}$	1.33	1.55	Single	O	Smells of burnt milk when heated.
Celluloid	2	1.35	1.50	Single	Tl	Easily flames.
Chalcedony	$6\frac{1}{2}$	2.62	1.53	Double	Tl	Sometimes used for carvings.
Chrysoberyl	$8\frac{1}{2}$	3.71	1.75–1.76	Double	T	Has less double refraction than zircon.
Diamond	10	3.52	2.42	Single	T	Tested by hardness and X-ray transparency.
Doublet	8	3.68	1.73	Single	T	Made of two pieces of synthetic white spinel.
Glass	6	V	V	Single	T	By internal bubbles and swirls.
Jasper	7	2.65	1.54	Double	O	Appearance and constants identify jasper.
Jadeite	7	3.34	1.66	Double	Tl	Shows a dimpled surface.
Nephrite	$6\frac{1}{2}$	3.00	1.61	Double	Tl	Brown nephrite due to weathering of green material.
Sapphire	9	3.99	1.76–1.77	Double	T	Many brown star sapphires are seen.
Scheelite	5	6.00	1.92–1.93	Double	T	Rare; but now made synthetically.
Sinhalite	$6\frac{1}{2}$	3.48	1.67–1.71	Double	T	Has large double refraction.
Soapstone	1	2.7	1.54	Double	O	Used for carvings, etc.
Sphene	$5\frac{1}{2}$	3.40	1.90–2.00	Double	T	Has much "fire" and large double refraction.
Topaz	8	3.53	1.63–1.64	Double	T	Distinguished from quartz by density.
Tourmaline	$7\frac{1}{2}$	3.08	1.62–1.64	Double	T	Distinguished from topaz by the larger double refraction.
Zircon	$7\frac{1}{2}$	4.68	1.92–1.98	Double	T	Doubling of the rear facets clearly seen.

LEGEND:—H.=Hardness; S.G.=Specific gravity; R.I.=Refractive indices; Ref.=Refraction; D.=Diaphaneity; V.=Variable; T.=Transparent; Tl.=Translucent; O.=Opaque.

Black Stones

	H.	S.G.	R.I.	Ref.	D.	Remarks
Bakelite	$2\frac{1}{2}$	1.28	1.65	Single	O	Smells of carbolic when touched with a hot needle.
Casein	$2\frac{1}{2}$	1.33	1.55	Single	O	Smells of burnt milk when touched with a hot needle.
Celluloid	2	1.35	1.50	Single	O	Flames when touched with a hot needle.
Coral	3	1.34	1.56	Single	O	This type of coral does not "fizz" with acid.
Diamond	10	3.52	2.42	Single	O	Tested by hardness and X-ray transparency.
Doublet	8	3.63	1.73	Single	O	Two pieces of white spinel with black layer.
Garnet	$6\frac{1}{2}$	3.7	1.89	Single	O	Melanite garnet conducts electricity.
Glass	6	V	V	Single	O	Chips show shell-like form.
Hematite	6	5.1	3.1	Double	O	Gives a red streak when rubbed on unglazed porcelain.
Jet	$3\frac{1}{2}$	1.33	1.66	Single	O	Smells of burning coal when heated.
Marble	3	2.71	1.50	Double	O	Effervesces with acid.
Obsidian	5	2.35	1.50	Single	O	Often shows a silvery schiller.
Onyx	$6\frac{1}{2}$	2.62	1.53	Double	O	Artificially stained chalcedony.
Opal	6	2.1	1.45	Single	Tl	Shows play of color.
Pearl	3	2.70	—	—	O	Lens shows surface to be made up of irregular lines.
Spinel	8	3.8	1.78	Single	O	Identified by density and refractive index.
Tourmaline	$7\frac{1}{4}$	3.2	1.65	Double	O	Usually shows only one shadow edge on the refractometer.
Vulcanite	$2\frac{1}{2}$	1.18	—	Single	O	Emits smell of burning rubber when heated.

LEGEND:—H.=Hardness; S.G.=Specific gravity; R.I.=Refractive indices; Ref.=Refraction; D.=Diaphaneity; V.=Variable; T.=Transparent; Tl.=Translucent; O.=Opaque.

Colorless Stones

	H.	S.G.	R.I.	Ref.	D.	Remarks
Beryl	$7\frac{1}{2}$	2.71	1.57–1.58	Double	T	Not an important stone.
Diamond	10	3.52	2.42	Single	T	Tested by its hardness and X-ray transparency.
Galliant (G.G.G.)	$6\frac{1}{2}$	7.05	2.03	Single	T	Peach colored glow under U.V. light.
Glass	6	V	V	Single	T	May have included bubbles.
Lithium niobate	$5\frac{1}{2}$	4.64	2.21–2.30	Double	T	Diamond simulant called Linobate.
Moonstone	6	2.55	1.52–1.53	Double	T	Often has bluish sheen.
Opal	6	2.10	1.45	Single	Tl	Often has a black matrix or is artificially blacked.
Phenacite	$7\frac{1}{2}$	2.96	1.65–1.67	Double	T	Identified by specific gravity and refractive index.
Rock crystal	7	2.65	1.54–1.55	Double	T	Also used for carvings.
Rutile (synthetic)	6	4.25	2.62–2.90	Double	T	Wide doubling of the back facets.
Sapphire (synthetic)	9	3.99	1.76–1.77	Double	T	By double refraction from synthetic white spinel.
Spinel (synthetic)	8	3.63	1.73	Single	T	Often used as a diamond imitation.
Strontium titanate	6	5.13	2.41	Single	T	Except for hardness good diamond simulant; called Fabulite and Diagem.
Topaz	8	3.56	1.61–1.62	Double	T	Has slippery feel.
Yttrium aluminate	8	4.57	1.83	Single	T	Simulates diamond and called Diamonair and Cirolite.
Yttrium oxide	8	4.84	1.92	Single	T	Simulates diamond.
Zircon	$7\frac{1}{2}$	4.68	1.92–1.98	Double	T	Doubling of the back facets readily seen.

LEGEND:—H.=Hardness; S.G.=Specific gravity; R.I.=Refractive indices; Ref.=Refraction; D.=Diaphaneity; V.=Variable; T.=Transparent; Tl.=Translucent; O.=Opaque.

Green Stones

	H.	S.G.	R.I.	Ref.	D.	Remarks
Alexandrite	$8\frac{1}{2}$	3.72	1.74–1.75	Double	T	Shows color change. Imitated by synthetic sapphire.
Amazonstone	$6\frac{1}{2}$	2.57	1.52–1.53	Double	Tl	Usually shows a schiller.
Aquamarine	$7\frac{1}{2}$	2.71	1.57–1.58	Double	T	Imitated by synthetic spinel and glass.
Aventurine quartz	7	2.65	1.54–1.55	Double	Tl	Identified by the included flakes of mica.
Bloodstone	7	2.62	1.53	Double	Tl	Dark green with red spots.
Bowenite	5	2.58	1.57	Double	Tl	Usually pale green with white feathery flecks.
Chrysoberyl	$8\frac{1}{2}$	3.72	1.74–1.75	Double	T	Also showing cat's-eye effect.
Chrysoprase	7	2.62	1.53	Double	Tl	Some chrysoprase is dyed chalcedony
Demantoid garnet	$6\frac{1}{2}$	3.84	1.88	Single	T	Lens shows asbestos fiber inclusions.
Diamond	10	3.52	2.42	Single	T	Rare in nature. Treated stones are often green.
Doublet (1)	7	2.7	1.54–1.55	Double	T	This is the "soudé emerald"; quartz and green layer.
Doublet (2)	8	3.7	1.73	Single	T	Consists of two pieces of synthetic spinel and green layer.
Doublet (3)	$7\frac{1}{2}$	2.7	1.57–1.58	Double	T	Consists of two pieces of green beryl and green layer.
Doublet (4)	$7\frac{1}{2}$	V	1.78	Single	T	Garnet top and glass base.
Eilat stone	5	2.8	1.50	—	O	A mixture of copper minerals.
Emerald	$7\frac{1}{2}$	2.69	1.57–1.58	Double	T	Usually red under the color filter, but not always.
Emerald (synthetic)	$7\frac{1}{2}$	2.65	1.55–1.56	Double	T	Very strong red under the color filter.
Fluorspar	4	3.18	1.43	Single	T	Often used for carvings and may look like beryl.
Glass	6	V	V	Single	T	Green under the color filter.
Grossular garnet	$7\frac{1}{4}$	3.63	1.74	Single	T	Varies from yellowish to emerald green.
Grossular garnet (massive)	7	3.45	1.72	Single	Tl	Has been miscalled "Transvaal jade."
Hiddenite	$6\frac{1}{2}$	3.18	1.66–1.67	Double	T	Large stones from Brazil.
Jadeite	7	3.34	1.65	Double	Tl	The so-called "Chinese jade."
Jasper	7	2.65	1.54–1.55	Double	O	Used as an ornamental stone.
Malachite	$3\frac{1}{2}$	3.8	—	Double	O	Banded. Fizzes with acid.
Nephrite	$6\frac{1}{2}$	3.0	1.61	Double	Tl	Lower S.G. than for jadeite.
Opal	6	2.1	1.45	Single	T	May look like chrysoprase but has lower density.
Peridot	$6\frac{1}{2}$	3.33	1.65–1.69	Double	T	Oil-green color and doubling of the back facets.
Quartz	7	2.65	1.54–1.55	Double	T	Either heat-treated amethyst or synthetic stone.
Sapphire	9	3.99	1.76–1.77	Double	T	Also made synthetically in this color.

continued

123

Green Stones *continued*

	H.	S.G.	R.I.	Ref.	D.	Remarks
Saussurite	6½	2.8–3.4	1.57–1.70	Double	Tl	A rock mixture of zoisite and albite. A jade imitation.
Soapstone	1	2.7	1.54	—	O	Used for native carvings.
Sphene	5½	3.40	1.90–2.00	Double	T	Identified by "fire" and large double refraction.
Spinel (synthetic)	8	3.63	1.73	Single	T	Differs from tourmaline by its single refraction.
Tourmaline	7½	3.08	1.62–1.64	Double	T	Imitated by synthetic spinel.
Turquoise	6	2.7	1.62	—	O	Not so prized as blue-colored stones.
Yttrium aluminate (Y.A.G.)	8	4.57	1.83	Single	T	Rare earth or chromium spectrum.
Zircon	6	4.1	1.80	—	T	Most green zircons are of the low type.

Violet Stones

	H.	S.G.	R.I.	Ref.	D.	Remarks
Almandine garnet	7½	4.2	1.79	Single	T	Its single refraction separates it from ruby.
Amethyst	7	2.65	1.54–1.55	Double	T	Often shows zonal coloration.
Doublet (1)	8	3.67	1.73	Single	T	The synthetic spinel doublet.
Doublet (2)	7½	V	1.78	Single	T	Garnet top on glass base.
Glass	6	V	V	Single	T	May show included bubbles.
Jadeite	7	3.34	1.65	Double	Tl	Shows a dimpled surface.
Kunzite	6½	3.18	1.66–1.67	Double	T	The lilac pink variety of spodumene.
Rhodolite garnet	7½	3.84	1.76	Single	T	Has a lovely rhododendron color.
Sapphire	9	3.99	1.76–1.77	Double	T	Is also made synthetically in this color.
Spinel	8	3.60	1.72	Single	T	Not made synthetically in this color.
Tourmaline	7½	3.08	1.62–1.64	Double	T	Sometimes known as siberite.

LEGEND:—H.=Hardness; S.G.=Specific gravity; R.I.=Refractive indices; Ref.=Refraction; D.=Diaphaneity; V.=Variable; T.=Transparent; Tl.=Translucent; O.=Opaque.

Blue Stones

	H.	S.G.	R.I.	Ref.	D.	Remarks
Aquamarine	$7\frac{1}{2}$	2.71	1.57–1.58	Double	T	Imitated by synthetic spinel and glass.
Chalcedony	$6\frac{1}{2}$	2.62	1.53	Double	T	May imitate some moonstones.
Diamond	10	3.52	2.42	Single	T	Natural colored stones conduct electricity.
Doublet (1)	8	3.69	1.73	Single	T	Synthetic white spinel top and base, with colored layer.
Doublet (2)	$7\frac{1}{2}$	V	1.78	Single	T	Garnet top and glass base.
Doublet (3)	9	3.99	1.77	Double	T	Natural sapphire top with synthetic sapphire base.
Eilat stone	5	2.8	1.50	—	O	A mixture of copper minerals.
Glass	6	V	V	Single	T	Bubbles and striae may be seen.
Iolite	7	2.61	1.53–1.54	Double	T	Lower specific gravity and refraction than sapphire.
Jadeite	7	3.34	1.65	Double	Tl	A rare color for jadeite.
Lapis lazuli	$5\frac{1}{2}$	2.85	1.50	Single	O	Usually shows specks of brassy pyrites.
Moonstone	6	2.55	1.53–1.54	Double	T	Beat stones show bluish flash.
Rutile	$6\frac{1}{2}$	4.25	2.62–2.90	Double	T	Synthetic stone showing large doubling of the back facets.
Sapphire	9	3.99	1.76–1.77	Double	T	The synthetic stones show curved banding.
Spinel	8	3.60	1.72	Single	T	Weak reddish under the color filter.
Spinel (synthetic)	8	3.63	1.73	Single	T	Strong red under the color filter.
Sodalite	$5\frac{1}{2}$	2.30	1.48	Single	O	Resembles lapis lazuli. Usually no pyrites.
"Swiss lapis"	$6\frac{1}{2}$	2.6	1.54	Double	O	Dyed jasper to imitate lapis lazuli.
Topaz	8	3.56	1.61–1.62	Double	T	Denser than aquamarine which it resembles.
Tourmaline	$7\frac{1}{2}$	3.08	1.62–1.64	Double	T	Doubling of the back facets readily seen.
Turquoise	6	2.7	1.62	—	O	Often waxed or treated.
Zircon	$7\frac{1}{2}$	4.68	1.92–1.98	Double	T	Strong doubling of the back facets can be seen.
Zoisite (Tanzanite)	6	3.35	1.69–1.70	Double	T	Has directional color changes of violet, blue and brown.

LEGEND:—H.=Hardness; S.G.=Specific gravity; R.I.=Refractive indices; Ref.=Refraction; D.=Diaphaneity; V.=Variable; T.=Transparent; Tl.=Translucent; O.=Opaque.

Red and Pink Stones

	H.	S.G.	R.I.	Ref.	D.	Remarks
Beryl	$7\frac{1}{2}$	2.71	1.57–1.58	Double	T	Also known as morganite.
Coral	$3\frac{1}{2}$	2.68	—	—	O	Effervesces with acid.
Conch pearl	$3\frac{1}{2}$	2.80	—	—	O	"Flame structure" on surface.
Cornelian	$6\frac{1}{2}$	2.62	1.53	Double	Tl	Usually stained chalcedony.
Diamond	10	3.52	2.42	Single	T	A very rare color of diamond.
Doublet (1)	$7\frac{1}{2}$	V	1.78	Single	T	Differences in relief of garnet-top and base identifies.
Doublet (2)	9	3.99	1.77	Double	T	Natural sapphire top with synthetic ruby base.
Fire opal	6	2.00	1.45	Single	T	Does not usually show a play-of-color.
Garnet	$7\frac{1}{2}$	3.8	1.79	Single	T	Garnet may vary in density and refractive index.
Glass	6	V	V	Single	T	May show bubbles and swirls.
Jadeite	7	3.34	1.66	Double	Tl	Shows a dimpled surface.
Jasper	7	2.65	1.54	Double	O	Identified by appearance and constants.
Kunzite	$6\frac{1}{2}$	3.18	1.66–1.67	Double	T	The lilac-pink variety of spodumene.
Rhodochrosite	4	3.6	1.8	Double	Tl	Usually banded. Used as an ornamental stone.
Rhodonite	6	3.54	1.72	Double	O	Harder than rhodochrosite and usually has black veins.
Rose quartz	7	2.65	1.54–1.55	Double	T	Often used for carved figures.
Ruby	9	3.99	1.76–1.77	Double	T	Distinguished from garnet by double refraction.
Rutile	$6\frac{1}{2}$	4.25	2.62–2.90	Double	T	Synthetic stone which shows large doubling of the back facets.
Spinel	8	3.60	1.72	Single	T	May be made synthetically, then has higher S.G. and R.I.
Topaz	8	3.53	1.63–1.64	Double	T	Distinguished from tourmaline by density.
Tourmaline	$7\frac{1}{4}$	3.08	1.62–1.64	Double	T	Distinguished from topaz by double refraction.
Zircon	$7\frac{1}{2}$	4.68	1.92–1.98	Double	T	Strong doubling of the back facets may be seen.

LEGEND:—H.=Hardness; S.G.=Specific gravity; R.I.=Refractive indices; Ref.=Refraction; D.=Diaphaneity; V.=Variable; T.=Transparent; Tl.=Translucent; O.=Opaque.

Orange and Yellow Stones

	H.	S.G.	R.I.	Ref.	D.	Remarks
Amber	$2\frac{1}{2}$	1.08	1.54	Single	T	The inclusion of insects is not proof.
Bakelite	$2\frac{1}{2}$	1.28	1.65	Single	T	Refractive index and density greater than for amber.
Beryl	$7\frac{1}{2}$	2.71	1.57–1.58	Double	T	Alternate name is heliodor.
Chalcedony	$6\frac{1}{2}$	2.62	1.53	Double	Tl	Usually stained.
Chrysoberyl	$8\frac{1}{2}$	3.72	1.74–1.75	Double	T	May show a cat's-eye effect.
Citrine	7	2.65	1.54–1.55	Double	T	Density and refractive index identifies.
Copal	$2\frac{1}{2}$	1.08	1.54	Single	T	Attacked by ether; amber is not easily.
Diamond	10	3.52	2.42	Single	T	Hardness and X-ray transparency test.
Doublet (1)	8	3.68	1.73	Single	T	Synthetic white spinel top and base.
Doublet (2)	$7\frac{1}{2}$	V	1.78	Single	T	Difference in luster of garnet top to glass base.
Fire opal	6	2.00	1.45	Single	T	Does not usually show a play of color.
Glass	6	V	V	Single	T	Shows conchoidal fracture and bubbles.
Hessonite	$7\frac{1}{4}$	3.65	1.74	Single	T	Generally full of bubble-like inclusions.
Jadeite	7	3.34	1.66	Double	Tl	Dimpled surface and density will identify.
Jasper	7	2.65	1.54	Double	O	Appearance usually tells this material.
Labradorite	6	2.69	1.56–1.57	Double	T	Transparent yellow labradorite is not often seen.
Orthoclase	6	2.56	1.53–1.54	Double	T	This orthoclase feldspar is not often seen.
Pyrites	6	5.00	—	—	O	Metallic luster. Used in jewelry as marcasite.
Sapphire	9	3.99	1.76–1.77	Double	T	Identified by density and refractive indices.
Scheelite	5	6.00	1.92–1.93	Double	T	Rare; but now made synthetically.
Spessartite	$7\frac{1}{4}$	4.2	1.81	Single	T	A rare garnet not often met in jewelry.
Sphene	$5\frac{1}{2}$	3.40	1.90–2.00	Double	T	Identified by its "fire" and double refraction.
Spinel	8	3.60	1.72	Single	T	Not a common color of spinel.
Spodumene	$6\frac{1}{2}$	3.18	1.66–1.67	Double	T	Rarely appears in jewelry.
Sinhalite	$6\frac{1}{2}$	3.48	1.67–1.71	Double	T	Has large double refraction.
Topaz	8	3.53	1.63–1.64	Double	T	Density greater than for tourmaline or citrine.
Tourmaline	$7\frac{1}{4}$	3.08	1.62–1.64	Double	T	Has greater double refraction than topaz.
Zircon	$7\frac{1}{2}$	4.68	1.92–1.98	Double	T	Doubling of the rear facets may be clearly seen.

LEGEND:—H.=Hardness; S.G.=Specific gravity; R.I.=Refractive indices; Ref.=Refraction; D.=Diaphaneity; V.=Variable; T.=Transparent; Tl.=Translucent; O.=Opaque.

Index

absorption spectrum, 117
achroite, 47
actinolite, 59
adamantine, 7
agalmanite, 89
agate, 75, 76–78
alabaster, 93
alexandrite, 50–51, D
Algerian onyx, 93
all-lapped method of producing
    cultured pearls, 106
alluvial sources, 8
almandite garnet, 42, C
Amazon-stone, 52
amber, 111–112
amethyst, 59, 60–61, 84, F
andalusite, 70
andradite, 45
Anne of Geierstein, 63
Antilles pearls, 109
anyolite, 33
apartheid, 38
apatite, 71, 116
aquamarine, 41, 84, B
"ashentrekker," 49
autoclave, 95
aventurine quartz, 62, 89
axestone, 85
axinite, 71
Aztec Indians, 82
azurmalachite, 90

baguettes, 21
bakelite, 96, 112
Balas rubies, 57
bandstone, 66
baroque, 42
baroque pearls, 103, 104, 107
batons, 21
benitoite, 71
beryls, 37–41, B
bezel facets, 25
"Big Hole," 10
birthstones, 84
Black Prince's Ruby, 57
blister pearl, 101, 102, 103, 105
bloodstone, 77, 84
Blue John spar, 92
bluestone, 92
bone, 84, 114, 115
boule, 95
bouton pearls, 103
bowenite, 88, 93
Brazilian emerald, 47
Brazilian onyx, 93
Brazilian peridot, 47
Brazilian sapphire, 47
Brazilian topaz, 46
brazilianite, 73
breccia, 93
brecciated agate, 78
brecciated jasper, 79
Bridgman, P. W., 7
brillianteerer, 25
Bristol diamond, 29
bruter, 25
Burmese rubies, 31, 33
byon, 31

cabochon cut, 5, 31, 34, 61
cacoxenite, 60
Cailliaud, F., 37
cairngorm, 59
calcite, 90, 91, 116
californite, 89
callais, 80
callaite, 80
cameos, 79, 114
canutillos, 37
carneol, 78
cascalho, 9
cassiterite, 73
catalyst, 7
cat's eye, 48, 49, 50, 51–52, 62,
    114, D
celluloid, 96
Central Selling Organization, 17
Central Sorting Office, 17
Ceylon chrysolite, 47
ceylonites, 57
chalcedony, 75–79, 89
chalcedony, coloring of, 78
chambering, 14
Chatham, Carroll F., 39
chatons, 96
chatoyant effect, 52, 70
Chelsea color filter, 38, 39, 78,
    117
cherry opal, 66
chert, 79, 91
chiastolite, 71
chicot pearls, 103
chlorastrolite, 73
chloromelanite, 86
chloropal, 68
chrysoberyl, 50–53, B, D
chrysocolla, 59, 73, 83
chrysolite, 56
chrysoprase, 75, 84, 89
cinnabar, 59, 77
Cirolite, 29
citrine, 59, 61, F
cleavage, 24, 46, 52
Cleopatra's mines, 37
cobalt, 60, 63, 108
composite stones, 96, 98, 117
conch, 101, 113, 114
conglomerate, 79
Connemara marble, 89
coque-de-perle, 110
coral, 78, 112–113
cordierite, 72
cornelian, 75, 78, 84
corundum, 31, 51, 57, A
Cristaria plicata, 105
crocidolite, 62
Crookes, William, 26
"crossed polars" position, 118
cross-worker, 25
crown, 19, 36
culet, 19
Cullinan Diamond, 24
cultured pearl, 105–110
cutting styles, 19, 24, 27, 34, 39,
    42, 51, 52, 54, 56, 60, 75, 77,
    83
cymophane, 50

cyst pearl, 101
Czochralski, 95

danburite, 71
demantoid garnet, 42, 44, 56
dendritic inclusions, 77
density, 116
dentine, 71, 114
Derbyshire spar, 92
Diagem, 29
Diamonair, 29
diamond, 7–29, 84, 116, E
    characteristics, 7
    classification, 17
    cutting and polishing, 18, 19,
        21–25
    formation, 7
    grading, 25
    recovery, 12–15, 17
    shapes, 17
    sources, 8, 9, 10, 11
diamond, atomic, 26
diamond, coloring of, 26, 27
diamond, effects under ultra-
    violet light, 26
diamond, industrial uses, 17, 28
diamond, largest cut in world,
    21
diamond, synthetics and simu-
    lants, 28, 29
diamond *grit,* 27
dichroic effect, 118
dichroism, 72
"dinny bone," 79
diopside, 71
dop, 25
double refraction, 34, 117
doublets, 96, 98
dullum, 33
dumortierite, 59

ear shell, 101
Ebelmen, J. J., 39
Eilat stone, 90
emeralds, 37–41, 84, A
    cutting and polishing, 38
    recovery, 37, 38
    sources, 37, 38
    synthetics and simulants,
        39–40
Emerita, 40
enstatite, 72
eosite, 62
epidote, 72
euclase, 72
Eureka Diamond, 9
Excelsior Diamond, 24

Fabergé, Carl, 58
Fabulite, 29, 95
facets, 27
faïence, 96
"feathers," 59–60
feldspar, 52–53, 116
fibrolite, 72
Finsch diamond mine, 8
fire, 19, 20, 21
fire opal, 66

firestones, 60
flame-fusion process, 95
float opal, 66
fluorspar, 92, 116
flux-fusion process, 95
fortification agate, 76
fossil wood, 68, 78
freshwater pearls, 102, 103

gahnite, 57
gahno-spinel, 57
garimpeiros, 9
garnets, 42–45, 84, 89, C
gemmologist, 116
gem-stick, 35
gemstone, characteristics, 5
General Electric Co., 28
gidgee opals, 68
girdle, 19
glass, 84, 96
Golconda district, 8
golden quartz, 60, 84, B
grading of gems, 30
graphite, 7
grossular garnet, 44
gypsum, 93, 116

Haliotis, 101
hardest substance known to man, 7
hauynite, 90
hawk's eye, 62
heat treatment to change color of stones, 41, 46, 47, 49, 54, 55, 60, 61, 78
hei tiki, 85
heliodor, 37
heliotrope, 77
hematite, 62, 110
Hertfordshire pudding stone, 79
hessonite, 44, 45, C
hiddenite, 70, D
Hope Diamond, 4, 7
howlite, 83
Hungarian opals, 66
hyalite, 66
hydrogrossular, 89
hydro-thermal process, 95
Hyropsis schegeli, 107

Idar-Oberstein, 76, 77
idocrase, 44, 72
illam, 33
imitation pearls, 108, 109
imitation stones, 96–97
Imperial green jade, 86
indicolite, 47, D
industrial diamond, 17
interference of light at thin films, 65
iolite, 72, C
iris agate, 78
iris quartz, 60
isomorphous, 42
ivory, 114
ivory simulants, 114–115

Jacob, Erasmus, 9
jadeite, 85, 86–88
jades, 85–89
Jagersfontein, 10
jamb-peg, 35
jargoon, 29, 54
jaspagate, 79

jasper, 75, 79
jaspillite, 79
jet, 112
Jonker Diamond, 26

Kashmir sapphires, 33
kerf, 24
Kimberley, 9
kimberlite, 10, 14
King Solomon's mines, 73
Koh-i-noor Diamond, 7
kornerupine, 73
kunzite, 61, 70, D
kyanite, 72

labradorite, 53
landscape agate, 76
lap, 35
lapidary-cut stones, 96
lapis lazuli, 79, 84, 90–92
laxy stone, 25
lazulite, 92
lenticles, 33
limonite, 81, 83
Linobate, 29
lucinite, 83
luminescence, 118

mabe pearls, 102, 105
macles, 24
"Madonna of the Star," 36
make, 25
malachite, 62, 90
mantle, 99, 101
Maori stone, 85
marble, 89, 93
marquises, 21
"mass aqua," 41
mawing, 87
maw-sit-sit, 88
meerschaum, 94
melt technique, 95
meres, 85
metamorphic rock, 62
metamorphosis, 90
microcline feldspar, 52
Mikimoto, Kokichi, 105
milky quartz, 61
mocha stone, 77
Mohs, 116
mollusks, 99, 101
moonstone, 52, 75, 84, C
morallons, 37
Morgan, J. P., 41
morganite, 37, 41
morion, 61
moss agates, 76–77
mother-of-pearl, 99, 103, 109
mtorodite, 75
mutton-fat jade, 85
myrickite, 77

nacre, 99, 101, 103
nacreous pearl, 101
navettes, 21
nephrite, 85–86
"new jade," 88
"nobbies," 67

odontolite, 83
olivene, 44
olivine, 44, 56
onyx, 93
onyx marble, 93

opal, 64–69, 84, C, E
opal dirt, 68
opal matrix, 68
opalescence, 65
opalite, 68
opercula, 114
organic gem materials, 99–115
orient, 104
ornamental stones, 90–94
over-blues, 25
oyster, 99, 101
oyster farms, 107

pastes, 35, 41, 57, 96
pavilion, 19, 36
pearl, 84, 99–110
pearl formation, 99, 101
pearl-sac, 101, 105
pearls, care of, 104, 108
pendeloque, 21
peridot, 46, 56–57, 84, C
petrified wood, 78, 79
phenakite, 71
piece method of creating cultured pearls, 106–107
piezo-electric effect, 59
Pinctada margaritifera, 101, 107
Pinctada martensi, 105, 107
Pinctada maxima, 101, 105, 107
Pinctada radiata, 101
pinite, 89
"pipes," 8, 13, 14
piqué marks, 109
piqué-work, 114
plasma, 59
plastics, 96
pleochroism, 34
polarized light, 117–118
polishing, 24
"pork-knockers," 9
potch, 66
prasiolite, 60
Project Mohole, 28
pseudomorphs, 78
pseudophite, 94
pulling technique, 95
pyrope garnet, 42, 43–44

quartz, 59–63
quartz-topaz, 46, 60
quartzite, 62

radio-activity, 54, 55
reef, 10
refraction of light, 56, 116
refractive index, 7
refractometer, 117, 118
reticulation, 42
rhodochrosite, 92
rhodolite garnet, 43, C
rhodonite, 92
ripple fracture, 60
rock crystal, 58, 59, 69, 71, 77, 84, 116
rondels, 59
rosée, 104
rough diamonds, 16, 17
rubellite, 47
rubies, 31–36, 84, A
ruin agate, 78
rutile, 59, 62

sagenitic agates, 77
Sandwana emeralds, 38

129

sapphires, 31–36, 84, 116, A
Sark stones, 60
saussurite, 88
scaife, 25
scapolite, 70
"schiller," 52, 61, 75
schorl, 47
scratch hardness scale of numbers, 116
scratch test, 116
sea shells, 114
seed pearls, 103
senaille, 19
sepiolite, 94
serpentine, 88, 93–94
"shincracker," 68
Siamese rubies, 33
siberite, 47
silica, 65
"silk," 34, 36
sillimanite, 72, 73
sinhalite, 57
sintering, 92
slurry, 14
smaragdus, 80
smithsonite, 73, 89
smoky quartz, 61, F
Snell's Law, 116
soapstone, 89, 94
sodalite, 90, 92
soudé stones, 40, 47, 51, 57, 60, 98, 117
spectroscope, 117
spessartite, 45, C
sphalerite, 74
sphene, 70, C
spinel, 57, D
spinel rubies, 57
spodumene, 70, D
staining, 78, 79, 84, 88, 91, 92, 111, 113

stalactites, 75
stalagmites, 75, 92
star effect, 34
Star of Africa, 21
Star of Sierra Leone, 24
starlite, 54
staurolite, 74
steatite, 94
stoping, 14
strass, 29
stripping, 34
Strombus gigas, 101
styles of cut, 6
Styrian jade, 94
sunstone, 53, D
surfacing, 34
Swiss lapis, 92
Symerald, 40
synthetic stone production, 95–96, 97

talc, 94, 116
tang, 25
tanzanite, 57, 71, 72, C
Tavernier, Jean Baptiste, 8
testing of gemstones, 29, 36, 40, 41, 42, 44, 47, 51, 57, 58, 61, 89, 92, 98, 109, 110, 112, 113, 114, 115, 116–118
teuxivitl, 82
Thetis'-hair stone, 59
thomsonite, 73
thulite, 57 5.5 (zoisite)
thunder egg, 78
tiger marking, 60
tiger's eye, 62
Timur Ruby, 57
tin-cut stones, 96
topaz, 46–47, 56, 84, 116, C
topazolites, 45

topaz-quartz, 46, 60
topographical agate, 76
tortoise-shell, 113–114
tourmaline, 47–49, B
Transvaal jade, 44
trapiche emerald, 37
tremolite, 85
triplets, 96, 98
triplex opals, 68
tumbling process, 42
turquoise, 80–84
twinlons, 31
twinned crystals, 74
Type 2B diamonds, 27

utahlite, 83

variscite, 83
Venus'-hair stone, 59
verdite, 89, 94
Verneuil, A., 36, 95

Wadi Maghareh, 81
wadis, 81
watermelon tourmalines, 48
water-opal, 66
Webster, Robert, 39
White Cliffs opal fields, 66, 67
williamsite, 94

xalostocite, 44
X-rays, 17, 118

YAG, 29

Zarnitza, 11
zinc-blende, 74
zircon, 54–55, B
zoisite, 55